"THE HIGHER CHRISTIAN LIFE"

SOURCES FOR THE STUDY OF THE HOLINESS, PENTECOSTAL, AND KESWICK MOVEMENTS

A forty-eight-volume
facsimile series reprinting
extremely rare documents for the study of
nineteenth-century religious and social history,
the rise of feminism, and the history of the
Pentecostal and Charismatic movements

Edited by
Donald W. Dayton
Northern Baptist Theological Seminary

Advisory Editors
D. William Faupel, *Asbury Theological Seminary*
Cecil M. Robeck, Jr., *Fuller Theological Seminary*
Gerald T. Sheppard, *Union Theological Seminary*

A GARLAND SERIES

KESWICK FROM WITHIN

J. B. Figgis

Garland Publishing, Inc.
New York & London
1985

For a complete list of the titles in this series
see the final pages of this volume.

Library of Congress Cataloging in Publication Data

Figgis, J. B.
KESWICK FROM WITHIN.

("The Higher Christian life")
Reprint. Originally published: London :
Marshall Bros., 1914.
Includes index.
1. Keswick movement I. Title. II. Series.
BV4487.K5F54 1985   270.8'1   84-25852
ISBN 0-8240-6417-8 (alk. paper)

The volumes in this series are printed on
acid-free, 250-year-life paper.

Printed in the United States of America

KESWICK FROM WITHIN

KESWICK FROM WITHIN

By the

REV. J. B. FIGGIS, M.A

Brighton

Author of "Christ and full Salvation,"
"Visions," etc.

With FOREWORD by the
RIGHT REV. THE BISHOP OF DURHAM

MARSHALL BROTHERS, LTD
LONDON EDINBURGH NEW YORK

BUTLER & TANNER,
THE SELWOOD PRINTING WORKS,
FROME, AND LONDON.

To the Old Guard
(on earth or in Heaven),
who for a generation and more
have led defeated souls
to victory
and restless souls to rest ;
this record of
forty years of mercies
is dedicated
by their unworthy comrade,

THE AUTHOR.

" Eunoë behold, that yonder rises ;
Lead him to it, and as thou art accustomed,
Revive again the half-dead virtue in him."

Purgatorio xxxiii.

" The time was come to drink of
Eunoë and *revive the memory of good.*"

A Shadow of Dante, by MARIA FRANCESCA ROSSETTI.

" In the time of Jerome the Church was not ashamed to seek instruction in the wilds of little Bethlehem.

" The learned Theology of to-day (though the parallel is not complete) might gather far more good than it is prepared to expect at the shores of the Cumbrian lake."

" *Religion in an Age of Doubt*," by Rev. CHARLES J. SHEBEARE, M.A.

PREFACE

" I BELIEVE in the communion of saints "—living saints and saints departed. Thus I count it one of the privileges of my life to know men, still, thank God, amongst us, who can tell of the origin of the Movement for the deepening of the Spiritual Life, a Movement which has meant so much for the Church of Christ in this and many lands. It was a joy to know also both the founders of the Keswick Convention, their poets—George Wade Robinson, Charles A. Fox, and Dr. Elder Cumming—and their predecessors, especially the gifted authoress of *The Christian's Secret of a Happy Life*. It was from her that the impulse to attempt this narrative came. In a letter to me in January, 1904, she said : " I wish you could see your way to writing a really full account of that wonderful Movement. I do not feel as if I could do it, because of being so intimately connected with it. But you, having been in it from the beginning and having so definitely experienced help and blessing by means of it, seem to be eminently fitted. I have, of course, Dr. Pierson's account, and also the Oxford and Brighton books, but I feel as if you could do something that neither of them has done."

Ten years have passed since Mrs. Pearsall Smith thus wrote, and as none of the leaders have found time to tell this wondrous story fully—and it did seem that some one of those connected with the Movement from its early days should recount its annals—I have ventured do try to be its chronicler. My book lays no claim to originality. It is almost a mosaic of the doings and the sayings of others. To recall them I have, no doubt, dived into memory, but I have also dived into memoirs and magazines, Dr. Harford's book[1] and

---

[1] *The Keswick Convention, its Message, its Method, and its Men* . A volume of exceptional value.

those Mrs. Smith refers to, besides the whole series of annual volumes of the KESWICK WEEK. Some visits have also been paid to Paternoster Row to find some missing link in an old *Christian* or *Life of Faith*. The search has been somewhat laborious, but it has been a labour of love. The treasures of spiritual thought and spiritual teaching contained in these many volumes have been " a possession for ever." One's only regret is that such a multitude of gems had to be left still immersed in forgotten tomes. Yet I hope enough has been rescued from oblivion to give a true picture of the holy scenes depicted. May those who have never visited them be able thus to visit them in spirit ! May those who have been there often, forgive the omission of probably the very utterances that helped them most ! And may " God, who is over all blessed for evermore," use this earnest but unworthy endeavour to show forth His praise !

J. B. FIGGIS.

BRIGHTON,
   January 25, 1914.

P.S.—A re-perusal of this volume makes me doubly conscious of its defects ; so much so as to make me feel that its great opportunity has by no means been reached. I see also that there are strange omissions. I have said very little of Mr. Head and Captain Tottenham, to whose admirable chairmanship we owe so much, both at Keswick and elsewhere. Nothing is recorded of some speakers and very little of others, able as they are, and dear friends also. I can only ask their forgiveness for this, and the indulgence of my readers for these and many blemishes.

J. B. F.

June 1, 1914.

FOREWORD

By H. C. G. MOULE, D.D., BISHOP OF DURHAM.

I WILLINGLY obey the desire of the honoured author, and write this brief prelude to KESWICK FROM WITHIN. Subject and writer alike command such service as I can render. The writer for many years has enriched me with his friendship in Christ, and no living person is better qualified to be the annalist of Keswick, intimate and understanding. The subject, the Convention, has been for the past thirty years and more one of the greatest and most formative spiritual interests of my life, at first as a problem suggesting misgiving and criticism, then recognized, in light given by God's grace, as the true, powerful, penetrating, Christian force which indeed it is.

The human, personal elements in the book are deeply moving to those who, like me, look far back to their first visit to the Convention. I turn the pages, and they are scattered over with the dear names of friends fallen asleep, and with memories of good days gone. But all along " life overwhelms death." They live with a great life above. And we have their true successors, living and witnessing below. And the hour of endless life, life together and with the Lord, draws on for both the circles.

HANDLEY DUNELM.

CONTENTS

3

CONTENTS

4

CONTENTS

CONTENTS

" Yes, I am happy now ;
    How easy was it all !
Just to cease struggling and allow
    My soul on Thee to fall ;
Just to be poor and weak,
    And all I really am,
Yet to have more than heart can seek
    In God's own perfect Lamb.

" Yes, I am happy now ;
    Though in myself alone
I still am nothing—only Thou
    Hast goodness of Thine own.
Oh ! Make it day by day
    Enough of joy for me,
That I, a worm of mortal clay,
    Have everything in Thee."

                         G. WADE ROBINSON.

CHAPTER I

" TWILIGHT "

THE doctrine of sanctification is as old as the Bible. In it flows a very river of life, the stream of pardon, and, from the same fountain of infinite grace, flows a river of purity and peace. On the title page of the New Testament we read that Jesus owed His Name to the fact that " He shall save His people from their sins." At the beginning of the history of the Church we read—" They were all filled with the Holy Ghost." In the epistles of St. Paul we have the prayer, " The very God of peace sanctify you wholly." In St. John's glorious letters, a central word is " Whosoever abideth in Him sinneth not," and the last epistle in Scripture has for its last word, " Now unto Him that is able to keep you from falling, and to present you faultless before the Presence of His glory with exceeding joy."

This pure stream from the River of the Water of Life has never failed in the Church of Christ. Sometimes it has been out of sight, but it has reappeared in a Francis de Sales or Thomas à Kempis. Molinos in his prison in Rome, Madame Guyon in the Bastille, were both channels through which this living river flowed. It flowed also through Marshall, the author of *The Gospel Mystery of Sanctification*, Fletcher, of Madeley, and many another friend of the Wesleys, and (perhaps unconsciously to themselves) through Jonathan Edwards and his devoted wife. Upham's works showed that the stream still ran on ; yet sixty years ago the publication of Boardman's *Higher Christian Life* created a sensation. Some said that it contained the seed of another Pentecost, others that there was enough error in it to poison a parish. On the whole, the favourable opinion prevailed, and not a few thus found their way to the banks of this River of purity and peace.

Grace for Grace, the letters of the Rev. William James, aided others. These books emanated from the Western World. America, which received such blessing long ago through our Whitefield and the Wesleys, sent to us blessings in return by the hands of Charles Finney, D. L. Moody, Robert Pearsall Smith and his admirable wife. He had remarkable gifts of attraction and inspiration, and Mrs. Smith (H. W. S.) had an intellectual grip of truth, and a life of confidence in God, that made her a glorious teacher and a sublime sufferer of quite unequalled influence. Her volume, *The Christian's Secret of a Happy Life*, with a wider circulation than any other book on holiness, had greater effect in leading pilgrims to this River than any other writing of any other man or woman of the time, with the possible exception of some of Miss Havergal's.

It is from her pen, too, that we have the record of the genesis of the Movement for the promotion of holiness in the last generation. In *The Unselfishness of God* she records the history of her personal adhesion to this Movement, and as the book is a large one and not perhaps very accessible, we think our readers will be grateful to us for an *outline* of this section of it.[1]

" In the year 1865 I had been a Christian nine years, but while I had found a religion that provided perfectly for my future deliverance, it did not seem to give me present deliverance. I was continually sinning and repenting, making good resolutions and breaking them, hating what was wrong and yet yielding to it ; longing for victory and sometimes getting it, but more often failing. I could not help seeing all the while that the Bible seemed to imply that Christ came to bring a real and present victory to His followers, but I was painfully conscious that I knew little of it. The fruits of the Spirit, which as a Christian I believed I had received, ' love. joy, peace, longsuffering, gentleness, goodness, faith, meekness, temperance '—these were just the things in which I knew myself to be deficient. . . . To be a child of God, and yet unable to act like one, made me wonder whether I had missed something which would have given me victory, and I determined to find out, if possible, what that something was. I questioned several older Christians about it, but from one and all I received the same answer :—' You have not missed anything ; the

---

[1] We think that the literary executors of H.W.S. would confer a great favour upon the Church of Christ if they would publish (say) in a shilling volume chapters xxv.–xxxii. of *The Unselfishness of God*. They are really a *separate* chapter in the autobiography of this gifted woman.

life of sinning and repenting is all that we can expect in this world, because of the weakness of the flesh.' . . . I continually cried with the Apostle, ' O wretched man that I am, who shall deliver me from the body of this death.' Yet the fact stared me in the face that Paul had not only asked that question but answered it, and said triumphantly, ' I thank God, through Jesus Christ our Lord.'

" Quaker examples around me seemed to say there must be deliverance somewhere. Again, a book given me by my father, *Spiritual Progress*, being a collection from the writings of Fénelon and Madame Guyon, gave me hope."

But hopes were counterbalanced by fears. . . . " I got into a most uncomfortable state, and began to be afraid that I was going to lose every bit of religion I possessed.

" There was a little dressmaker in the village to which we had removed. She told me that her people taught ' The Doctrine of Holiness,' and that there was an experience called ' Sanctification,' or ' The Second Blessing,' which brought you into a place of victory. At last I made up my mind to give a meeting she spoke of the favour of my presence. I went, thinking it very likely I should astonish them by my Biblical knowledge. When I entered the meeting a factory woman was speaking, and I heard her say, ' My whole horizon used to be filled with this great big ME, but when I got a sight of Christ, as my perfect Saviour, this great big ME wilted down to nothing.' These words were a revelation to me. . . . Needless to say, I did not undertake to do any teaching that night, but sat as a learner at the feet of these humble Christians, who knew but little book-learning, but whose souls were evidently taught of the Spirit.

" I entered in my diary : ' I find there are some Christians who say that by receiving Christ by faith for our sanctification, just as we received Him by faith for our justification, all that I long for is accomplished. . . . That the Bible teaches that the Lord can deliver from the power of sin, as well as from its guilt, and the soul learns to trust Him to do it and to cease to rely upon resolutions or efforts. I begin to see that the Lord is worthy of my boundless confidence.' "

A year later the diary records :—" The present attitude of my soul is that of trust in the Lord, and I have found it a practical reality that He does deliver. When temptation comes, if I turn at once to Him, breathing this prayer, ' Lord, save me, I cannot save myself from this sin, but Thou canst and wilt,' He never fails me. Either He changes my feelings in the case, or He causes me to forget all about it, and my victory, or rather His victory, is entire. This is a secret of the Christian life which I never knew before.

" Now I commit my daily life to Him, as well as my future destiny, and I trust Him just as nakedly for the one as for the other. I am equally powerless in both cases. I can do nothing—not even I, the New Man—and if the Lord does not do it all, it will not be done, but oh ! glorious truth, He does do it. When I trust Him He gives me deliverance from the power of sin, as well as from its guilt. I can leave all things in His care—my cares, my temptations, my growth, my service, my daily life, moment by moment. Oh ! the rest and calm of a life like this. . . . And this is the Methodist Blessing of Holiness, couched by them, it is true, in terms that I cannot altogether endorse, and held amid, what seems to me, a mixture of error, but still really and livingly experienced and enjoyed by them !

"Every page of the Bible now seemed to declare in trumpet tones the reality of a victorious and triumphant life to be lived by faith in the Lord Jesus Christ. My whole soul was afire with my discovery, I could scarcely think or talk of anything else."

But she not only taught the Blessing, she lived it. "The practical working of my new discovery amazed me. I committed the whole matter of my rebellious spirit to the Lord and told Him I could not conquer it, but that I believed that He could conquer it for me ; and then I stood aside, as it were, and left the battle to Him, and to my indescribable joy, I found all my rebellion taken away, and the life which had before looked so distasteful, began to look pleasant and even desirable."

She tells of a case in which she had been imposed upon. She rushed to her room, knelt down, and said, "Lord, I am provoked, I want to be provoked, and I think I have cause for being provoked ; but I know I ought not to be, and I want the victory. I hand this whole matter over to Thee. ' Jesus saves me now.' According to experience I was declaring a lie, when I said this, for I was not saved, I was brim full of rebellion ; but by faith I laid hold of victory and the result was that immediately a summer morning of peace and happiness spread over me and I felt as happy as a bird. Many hundreds of battles have been fought and won for me since by the Captain of my Salvation, and the secret I learned then of handing over the battle to the Lord and leaving it in His hands, has never failed to work, when I have acted on it. The Lord Jesus is not dead, but ' ever liveth to make intercession for us.' I had discovered that *faith is the conquering law of the universe.* A wonderful light streamed upon 1 John v. 14, 15, ' If we know that He hears us we know that we have the petitions that we desire of Him ! ' I had thought of this passage as a beautiful dream, now I saw it was no dream, but a statement of a Divine law, the law of faith, a law as certain as the law of gravitation. I saw that *faith links us to the Almighty power of God*, so there seemed no limit to its possibilities.

"I wish I could say that I have always since lived in the power of this Divine law, but one thing I can say, that whenever and wherever I have chosen to lay hold by faith of God's strength, it has always been made ' perfect in ' my ' weakness,' and I have had the victory.

"At first my husband felt somewhat frightened. He continually fell back on the argument that the ' old man ' must always bring us into bondage. ' Impossible or not,' I said, ' it is certainly in the Bible, and I would like to know what thee thinks of Romans vi. 6. What can this mean but that the power of sin is really to be conquered, so that we no longer need to serve sin.' Startled, he exclaimed, ' There is no such passage in the Bible.' ' Oh ! yes there is,' I replied, and turning to my Bible I showed it to him. With the verse, of course, he had been familiar, but it now appeared as if he had never seen it before. It brought conviction, however, and from that time he did not rest until he had discovered the truth for himself."

So R. P. S. tells us in an account of this discovery, published in 1868, " Romans vi. 6 certainly must mean something and something which would make it possible for a believer no longer to be a slave of sin. . . . ' Is that all you mean ? ' I asked when this had been specially pressed upon me. ' That is nothing new, I have always known it.' ' But have you lived it ? ' was the question. ' Yes,' I replied, ' often.' ' You have realized it as an occasional experience,' was the answer, ' but have you realized it as a life ? You say you have taken refuge in the Lord sometimes, but have you ever taken up your abode in Him ? ' I saw that I had not ; my faith had been very intermittent in this respect. In circumstances of peculiar difficulty I had had recourse to the Lord, but that this occasional experience might be, and ought to be, the experience of my whole life, I had never dreamed. ' What would you think,' asked my friend, ' of people who should trust Christ in this intermittent way for the salvation of their souls ? ' . . . ' Is it not equally inconsistent and dishonouring to the Lord to trust Him for your daily living in this intermittent way, sometimes walking by faith and sometimes by your own efforts ? ' I could not but acknowledge the truth of this, and the possibility and blessedness of a life of continual faith began to dawn upon me."

So, resumes his wife's record :—" We were from this time forward of one accord in regard to this. It was not that either he or I considered ourselves to have become sinless, or that we never met with any further failures. We had simply discovered the Secret of Victory, and knew that we might, if we would, be made more than conquerors through our Lord Jesus Christ. When we neglected to avail ourselves of the ' Secret,' and, instead of handing the battle over to the Lord, took it into our own hands, as of old, failure inevitably followed."

Hannah Smith soon discovered that the life of faith was a Quaker doctrine. " My dear father, who was a genuine Quaker, as well as a most delightful one, owned to it. At the earliest opportunity I told him of our new discovery, and said, ' And now, father, is not this the secret of thy life and the source of thy strength ? Is not this the way thou hast always lived ? ' I shall never forget his reply. ' Why, of course it is, daughter,' he said, with a joyous ring of triumph in his voice ; ' I know of no other way to live, and I do know,' he added reverently, ' what it is, when the enemy comes in like a flood, for the Spirit of the Lord to lift up a standard against him.' But I must confess that although we found that the Friends did actually teach it, yet it was among the Methodists that we received the clearest light. Especially did we enjoy their Camp Meetings.

" An unexpected visitor, seeking us in our tent at one of them, met the people returning from the early Prayer Meeting. He was profoundly impressed " (just as people are at Keswick to-day) " with their looks of peace and joy, and he said, ' What makes their faces shine so ? ' We told him that these were an index of hearts at rest in the Lord. ' Well,' he said, ' I am determined that I, too, will get a shining face, and will stay on in this Camp till I do.' In a few days his face, also, was shining with the joy of God.

" The truth came to me with intellectual conviction and delight ; my husband, being more of an emotional nature, received the Blessing in true Methodist fashion, and came home full of Divine glow. He said he had retired to the woods to continue the prayer by himself. The whole world seemed transformed to him. This ecstasy lasted for weeks, and was the beginning of a wonderful career of power and blessing. I confess I was rather jealous that I had not received like ' Blessing,' and I renewed my efforts to obtain it. But it was all in vain ; I never seemed to get out of the region of conviction into the region of emotion. I became convinced at last that the reason of this difference of experience was not that others were peculiarly favoured by God above me, but that their emotional natures received with emotional delight the same truths that I received calmly."

Yet she speaks of having entered upon " a region of romance before which all other romances paled." " It was like an exploration of the very Courts of Heaven itself. . . . I can understand the joy with which the Psalmist reiterated, ' O, that men would praise the Lord for His goodness.' I can never put into words all that I begin to see of the loveliness, tenderness, unselfishness, infinite goodness of the Will of God. The reason Heaven is Heaven is because God's Will is perfectly done there, and earth would be like Heaven if it were perfectly done here. An old writer has said that ' God's Will is not a load to carry but a pillow to rest on,' and I have found that this is true." And so she found to the end. " I am now seventy years old ; old age with its failing powers and many infirmities without God could not but be sad and wearisome, but with God, our lovely unselfish God, old age is simply a delightful resting-place."

Ten years later this happy soul made to itself wings and flew away to God's happy Heaven, and there with a song (surely no angel's can be sweeter !) she sings of God's eternal love and power and joy.

So God was preparing sowers to go forth into the fields bearing precious seed. In one school after another they had been acquiring teaching, very deep and very practical. They had had discernment enough also to separate the chaff from the wheat, and with their seed basket full and running over, they crossed the Atlantic to bring to Europe, and especially to these islands, " the seed of peace " and " the fruit of good living to the praise and glory of God's Holy Name."

CHAPTER II

" DAYBREAK "

THE BROADLANDS CONFERENCE

" We were a people of God's gathering. We wanted the presence and power of His Spirit to be inwardly manifested in our spirits. We had (as I may say) what we could gather from the letter, and endeavoured to practise what we could read in the letter, but we wanted ' power from on high,' we wanted life, we wanted the Presence and fellowship of our Beloved, we wanted the knowledge of the Heavenly Seed of the Kingdom and an entrance into it, and the holy dominion and reign of the Lord of Life over the flesh, over sin, and over death in us. . . . And who can utter what the glow of the Light was in its shining and breaking forth in our hearts ! Oh ! the joy of that day wherein we sensibly felt the pouring down of the Spirit of Life upon us, and our hearts gathered into the bosom of Eternal rest, and our souls and bodies sanctified and set apart for the Lord and His service."

ISAAC PENNINGTON.

THE scene shifts from America to Europe, and from a little village to the great city.

" Shall I ever forget," writes the Rev. E. W. Moore,[1] " the meeting in London on May 1, 1873, attended by about sixteen persons, five or six of whom remain unto this present, but the rest are fallen asleep, at which a servant of Christ arose and, instead of, as I feared, propounding some new theology, gave the simple testimony that ' A great blessing had come into his life through deep searchings of heart.' Simple as the testimony was, it proved quick and powerful to some who heard it, and from that little meeting, as from an obscure source and spring, the stream of Keswick teaching and influence, which has gone round the world since then, may truly be said to have taken its rise."

Mr. Moore's " brother and companion " in this gracious Move-

[1] *Keswick Convention*, edited by Dr. Harford.

15

ment, the Rev. Evan Hopkins, writes in the same volume:
"During the year 1873 small meetings were held in London.
Here great and Divine blessings were realized by a few.
Then followed larger gatherings, and in 1874 special Union
Meetings for Consecration, for two or three days at a time,
were held at the Mildmay Conference Hall, at Hanover Square
Rooms, and in other places. Similar Conferences were held
in Dublin, Nottingham and Leicester; on the Continent, too,
meetings for the same purpose and on exactly similar lines
were held and largely attended. . . .

"So sudden and striking were the transformations that
took place in the experiences and life of some of God's most
earnest workers, that even those who regarded the Movement
with suspicion were unable to gainsay the reality of the
blessings that followed."

One of those privileged in the earliest period to experience
this grace of God, and that in an eminent degree, was Miss
Caroline Hanbury (afterwards Mrs. Albert Head). She enters
in her diary, June 15, 1873, the year in which "our dear,
beloved Mr. Pennefather went in to see the King": "How
can I write the blessing to myself of the last few weeks. Oh,
that it may ever be 'Not I, but Christ liveth in me.' I cannot
stand one moment alone, but He can keep me." And to her
sister she writes: "My experience seems just 'love, joy
peace,' all day long. Everything goes right, doesn't it?"

On June 9 these sisters and their aunt set out for
Switzerland, where they had two months of learning more
of the joy of entire consecration from Mr. Pearsall Smith;
and also at the Riffel they met Mr. Hackett, Mr. Hopkins,
Mr. Moore and others, and spent ten days "in waiting upon
God."

Again at Chamonix they found a quiet and beautiful spot
where "every one of them was at liberty in His Presence to
enjoy either Bible reading, hymn singing, prayer or expedi-
tions." The writer especially recalls little gatherings for
"waiting on Him" held in the wood among trees and rocks
with the glistening snows of Mont Blanc just above.

"And now I must tell you," wrote the subject of this bright
biography, "'He is able'; I have proved it again and again.
Jesus has made Himself to me a living, bright reality. He

carries me with all my burdens, trials, cares and sins, and I
have no longer to carry them myself. Of course there are
temptations and things to vex and try one as much as ever,
but when I give the battle up to Jesus, He always conquers."
To few friends was the Movement more indebted in its
early days than to the family of Sir Thomas Beauchamp, of
Langley Park, Norfolk. His daughter, Mrs. Drury-Lowe, in
a recent letter to Miss Nugent writes : " My grandmother,
Lady Radstock,[1] was always in touch with those who were
pressing on in spiritual apprehension, and kept my father
and mother in touch with them too. Living in London, she
had met the Boardmans, who had come down to us some-
time before the Pearsall Smiths came to England, and they
had been much interested in his book, *The Higher Christian
Life*. The other friends followed on, and so the succeeding
links were forged. I believe that Mr. Pearsall Smith's visit
there was one of the preliminary links in the evolution of
the Keswick Convention ; he came there first of all (in November, 1873 ?) with his wife, and also Mr. and Mrs. Boardman,
if I remember rightly, Mr. Moore (E. W.),[2] and Mr. Evan
Hopkins were there then, and they met many of our lay and
clerical neighbours. In the following June or July my father
and mother arranged to fill the house to its utmost capacity,
for the inside of a week. Besides those already named I
think Mr. Fox, Mr. and Mrs. Filmer Sulivan, and Mr. and
Lady Alice Sherbrooke were present. It proved to be a very
hallowed time, with a hush of solemnity over it, as, only two
months before, Sir James Paget had told my father that he
had internal trouble that would probably end fatally in six
months' time. During the Conference no one would have
known there was anything the matter with him, but in the
first week in October he passed away. I always understood
that the question of the Oxford Convention was decided there,
and that Keswick was an outcome of the Oxford Convention.
I feel my grasp of the details of the Conference itself was very
limited, as the burden of my father's condition and a very
full house kept my mind very fully occupied." Fuller details

[1] The mother of the Lord Radstock known to many of our readers,
and so recently translated.

[2] Not at this first, but at the later and larger Conference.

of these Langley Park gatherings are among the beautiful secrets which may be told in the world beyond the grave. The extension of such experiences to a larger number was greatly due to a Conference held at Broadlands, near Romsey, the stately Hampshire home of Lord Mount-Temple. A wish had been expressed that meetings of a somewhat similar type to the Camp Meetings in America, alluded to in the previous chapter, should be held in England. " I will gladly lend Broadlands for such a purpose," said Mr. Cowper-Temple, as he then was. About a hundred persons drew together to that sweet retreat for a Conference of six days in the July of 1874. Mr. Hopkins tells a little about this Conference in his chapter on "Preliminary Stages" in Dr. Harford's book, but "Broadlands" has a whole volume to itself, *The Life that is Life Indeed*, by Miss Edna Jackson. Deeply interesting is her chapter "Personalities," beginning with Lord Mount-Temple, the son of Earl Cowper, and his beautiful wife, the sister of Lord Melbourne, once Prime Minister. Mr. Cowper-Temple's mother subsequently married Lord Palmerston, and the striking portrait of the statesman looked down upon the guests.

He used to hold meetings in the New Forest, "and speak to the people from a cottage window or court, so anxious was he to bring them to the knowledge of God." Lady Mount-Temple, speaking of their forty years of happy wedded life, says : " I cannot remember the slightest lapse from his perfect trust in God and daily devotion to his Master. I never detected the least film on the crystal clearness of his sincerity. I never saw a ruffle on his serene and sweet temper. I never knew him fail in sympathy."

Lady Mount-Temple,[1] whom in her girlhood Ruskin saw in Rome, "and although he never succeeded in getting within many yards of her, she was the light and solace of that Roman winter to him." And later, after her marriage, she became "a tutelary power of the brightest and happiest," to him.

> " Sunshine was she in the wintry day,
>   And in the mid-summer, coolness and shade."

---

[1] See her portrait in Hon. Lionel Tollemache's Autobiography.

"Among the speakers," writes Miss Jackson, "I think first of Mrs. Pearsall Smith, ' The Angel of the Churches,' as Lady Mount-Temple called her." " Can we ever forget," says Mrs. Russell Gurney, "the early morning when she stepped forward from the shade with the simplicity and dignity of a queenly child, saying, ' I want to say something, Robert,' and then, with her sun-illuminated countenance turned upon us, began, ' I want to tell you, dear friends, of the joy this communion with the Lord gives, never mind under what circumstances. I have seen it, I have known it.' Then she urged us to prove for ourselves the blessedness of yielding unreservedly to God, that He might work in us ' to will and to do of His good pleasure.' "

Other speakers at "Broadlands" were Canon (now Archdeacon) Wilberforce ; the Rev. Andrew Jukes ; George Mac-Donald, of whom his college professor said "that there was more imagination in his little finger than in the whole bodies of all the rest of the college put together " ; Mr. Clifford, who in 1888 went to visit Father Damien on the Leper Island ; the Rev. Wilson Carlile, "now the valued and indefatigable head of the Church Army " ; Stanley Smith, the athlete, who like the wonderful Senior Wrangler, Henry Martyn, had gone to the heathen ; and another missionary, the Honourable Ion Keith-Falconer ; John Pulsford, the mystic ; and above all, Theodore Monod." The book speaks of "his rapt face and eyes with all the tragedy of France in them." No one that heard this gifted young Frenchman in those days can forget the deep impression that he made. No one that has joined in his hymn, " Oh ! the bitter shame and sorrow," which was written there and then, can fail to feel that the Continent of Europe, as well as the Continent of America, had contributed a rich spiritual gift to the Christian life of this England of ours.

There were striking women speakers, besides Hannah Smith —as her chosen friends loved to call her. Miss Marsh, the authoress of the *Life of Hedley Vicars* and *English Hearts and English Hands,* was present at some of the Conferences and conducted some of the English services in the Park. Antoinette Sterling came with her beautiful voice and beautiful heart to help others, who felt as she had felt when a girl of eighteen, when she said, "I have an ardour to be good and to do good, to be noble in thought and deed."

Another and very different sister, also a singer in her way, was present and spoke at one of the Broadlands Conferences— the Christian negress, Amanda Smith. Born in Cincinnati in 1837, and the child of slave parents, "she had," said Bishop Thorburn, of Calcutta, "that indefinable something we call power. During the seventeen years I have lived in Calcutta I have known many famous strangers to visit the city, some of whom attracted large audiences, but I have never known any one who could draw and hold so large an audience as Mrs. Amanda Smith. The manager of the theatre said 'I would do anything for that inspired woman;'" and, the bishop wrote in 1891—"She is gratefully remembered by thousands in India, Indians as well as English. She bore herself with the dignity of a 'king's daughter' and the simplicity of a little child. After the meeting, Lady Mount-Temple met her in the hall, put her arms round her and kissed her before all the people, and Lord Mount-Temple gave her his arm and led her in to dinner, where he seated her at his right hand."

Others might be mentioned who flit to and fro on the pages of this volume; but after all it was not the people, it was the teaching that riveted the gathering and kindled and sustained its interest. There seemed to be a Voice above the waving trees of the Park, the "still small voice of God," saying "Behold, I will do a new thing," and not a few of that company who had come thither jaded, perplexed, defeated, "disgusted with themselves," as one frankly phrased it, went away calm, quiet, humble but happy in the possession in their hearts and lives of a reigning God and conquering Christ. As to God's Will, they had learned that it was absolute and perfect love. As to God's power, they had learned that it was omnipotence.

"Broadlands" was fragrant with the breath of a heavenly morning, and many a soul left it full of morning joy.

CHAPTER III

THE SPRING OF THE DAY

" Around us Oxford, dome and tower,
　　Majestic, breathed the charm august ;
　But which of all her spells had power
　　To raise the wretched from the dust ?

" What Oxford could not, Jesus did,
　　Bared to my eyes the depths of grace,
　And all the unguessed treasures hid
　　Beneath the dust of commonplace.

" Since then, I tread the pilgrim's way,
　　Still plodding on through sun and rain,
　But like a star shines out that day—
　　The day which saw me born again."
　　　　　　C. FIELD, on *The Commonwealth.*

WHOEVER wishes to understand the true inwardness
of the Keswick Movement should read the *Account
of the Union Meeting for the Promotion of Scriptural Holiness
held at Oxford August 29 to September 7*, 1874.

In that small volume he will find testimonies of holy men and
women long since numbered with the " saints in glory everlasting," and of a few still left to witness to God's grace and
power. He will find too the principles they enunciated, the
purposes that united them in an agreement never seen before
and rarely since. The purpose of those who gathered was
to seek " the fulness of the blessing of the Gospel of
Christ." The principles were that full blessing, like every
other part of the great " Salvation, is of the Lord " : and
that to enjoy full blessing there must be full surrender, and
sincere faith.

In the perusal of the record one is struck with the number
of speakers who at times took part in the meetings. It was

a true Conference, inasmuch as we were evidently assembled
to confer.

We who went to Oxford " had heard in the country of Moab
how that the Lord had visited His people in giving them bread."
" People tell us "—in words that Dr. Dale, speaking a year
after at a meeting of the Congregational Union, used in describ-
ing the experience—that " they have come to see a larger
power in God for the sanctification of the soul than they had
ever imagined before. Is not that a good thing for any Christian man to discover ? We all rely on the power of God to
sanctify us, and they say that they have discovered that that
power can be more completely trusted than they had before
suspected. I think that is a happy discovery for them : and
if the same discovery can be made to me, I shall thank God
for making it to me." And he added, illustrating his point
fully, " We ought to make people understand that, if the Grace
of God can cure drunkenness, it can cure a bad temper. My
impression is that the substance of the teaching is that God
is as able to save men from one set of sins as from another."

Christians had come to Oxford in dead earnest to obtain
this grace, and the language of soul after soul was that of
wrestling Jacob. " I will not let Thee go except Thou bless
me," and as truly it might be added, " He blessed him there."

I had the privilege of being one of four[1] Brighton ministers
who were present.

Who is there for whom Oxford has not a charm ? Its Col-
leges, hoary with age and beautiful at that season with the
deeply tinted Virginian creeper ; its churches, especially that
of St. Mary the Virgin, which had echoed to the voice of John
Henry Newman, and many another mighty preacher ; these
and the fair outline of what Dean Stanley regarded as the
finest street in England—" The High "—the venerable pile
of the Sheldonian Theatre, of Christ Church, and of the
College, where the Prince of Wales is a student, seen from
the Bridge of Magdalen : all cast their spell over the ordinary
traveller. But the hundreds who came up to the Convention
were no ordinary travellers, and for them Oxford was as unlike
the Oxford of the Schools, the Union and the boats, as any-

---

[1] The others were the Rev. Filmer Sulivan, his helper, Rev. David
Graham, and the Rev. G. Wade Robinson.

thing could be ; but surely it was very like the Oxford of
Whitefield, and the Wesleys, and " the Holy Club." The same
walls, in the nineteenth as in the eighteeneth century, looked
down on men animated by the same purpose—the purpose to
live a life wholly for God. But there was this great difference.
Whitefield and the Wesleys, at that early stage of their career,
did not know that Salvation is of *faith*, not of works. Those
who gathered to the Convention knew this well ; yet many
of them were labouring under a similar mistake, for they did
not know that sanctification, like justification, was a blessing
obtainable by simple *faith*. This was the truth they had
come to Oxford to learn.

Amongst the speakers were men from many countries. Dr.
Mahan, formerly Principal of Oberlin, Rev. W. E. Boardman,
and Mr. and Mrs. Pearsall Smith, who captivated us by their
telling words and their winning ways,—these came from
America. Pasteurs Theodore Monod, Fisch and others came from
France ; Pastor Rappard, head of the Missionary College at
Crischona, Professor Bovay, Pastor Stockmeyer, and M. Gobat
from Switzerland ; Baron von Gemmingen, Professors Vernier
and Müller, and others from Germany ; the Hon. P. J. Elout
de Loeterwonde, and the Hon. J. W. Van Loome from Holland.
The list of speakers from England would be far too long to
give.

The day commenced with a Prayer Meeting at 7 a.m.
" The streets of Oxford formed truly a striking scene ; from
eight hundred to a thousand[1] persons passing through them
at this early hour, with the quiet earnestness of purpose
depicted in their countenances. It is impossible to put into
words the quiet sweetness and sense of the presence of Christ
during those early hours. The simple reading of Scripture,
or the responsive repetition of a Psalm, seemed to thrill and
penetrate the assembly more than an eloquent address usually
does."

Almost as informal were the general morning meetings,
and, at least, the ministerial meetings each afternoon. But
there were other portions of the day at which some special
speaker had the whole attention of the audience. This was
especially the case at 3 o'clock each afternoon, when Mrs.

---

[1] I think that these numbers are exaggerated.

Pearsall Smith gave a Bible Reading. Anything more impressive or delightful, now sparkling with humour, now touching to tears, than this series of addresses we never remember hearing.

" If some one should come and say the Lord Jesus is in your house, this room would be cleared in two minutes. Some would go for joy at His presence, some perhaps to get something out of the way before He should see it."

" Our heaviest care is the care of ourselves, and even this He relieves us from. Who can manage things best, you or the Lord ? You can trust Him to manage the universe, why not your life ? Have you ever thought how astonished the angels must be at our ignorance and indifference about our amazing privileges ? They see us beggars where we ought to be millionaires ; they see us serving, where we ought to reign ; they see us starving, where we ought to be satisfied with marrow and fatness." " Tell the Lord that you *will* keep His law, and He immediately takes possession of you and says, ' Yes you *shall*.' He does it all, and your part is to surrender, His to take that which you surrender. He only wants you to say ' yes ' to Him. Intensely do I long that there should be something *done* here to-day, as well as something talked about."

The words of the leader are given more fully in this volume, and they are very beautiful, some of them very pathetic, for he told us how there came " a fall upon his head causing congestion of the brain and suffering the physicians said never exceeded in their experience." [1]

" In the interior of South America, alone, and weeks away from Christian communion, instead of health I found yet deeper depths, and in their midst the powerful assaults of Satan, suggesting even infidelity. To all his attacks I said, I will believe, live or die, in agony or joy, I will believe." From such intense assaults came the power to lend a helping hand to many a struggler in the storm of temptation. He told of one urged to surrender. " I cannot, the step would be worse than death to me." " Better die than disobey God," I replied ;

---

[1] These words of R. P. S. go a good way to explain the breakdown which deprived later Conventions of his presence.

'the early Christians did.' And after a time, this shadow, that overcast his ministry, was lifted from his life."

"We read of the *works* of the flesh, but of the *fruit* of the spirit. Do not try to make fruit, but place yourself in the beams of the Sun of Righteousness and let *it* ripen all heavenly fruit in you." "Are you sweet at home—tender and Christ-like? Does the sudden pull of the bell ever give notice in the kitchen that a good temper has been lost by the head of the household? Trust Christ first at home and remember that His personal nearness is as real as it was in the sacred home at Bethany."

"I once brought some peaches to a suffering *Southern* soldier. He burst into tears : 'Your kindness breaks my heart,' he said. Can you not let grace break your heart and accept its wealth of privilege ?"

"For twenty years there has been running through my heart these words : '*I've none to please but Jesus.*' As a wife would seek to please her husband, so please HIM."

"If you have rest, you have not worry ; if you have worry, you have not rest. The trusting heart hears the word— 'Thy soul shall dwell at ease.' God is your Father, your Heavenly Father ; can He make His obedient child miserable ?"

"Avoid judging ; my views are what I am able to *see*— nothing more. I am not a pope—nor you either, my dog-matic friend. Seated with Christ in heavenly places, I am sure to be humbled by my ignorance."

Contrary to the impression once very prevalent that Mr. Smith taught sinless perfection, he is expressly stated to have said : "Our teaching is the exact antithesis of perfection in the flesh. In the flesh dwelleth no good thing, nor ever will. It was judged and condemned in the Cross of Christ. As the Articles of the Church of England truly say, 'This infection of nature doth remain, yea in them that are regenerate.' We should tremble to lead any one beyond saying daily, 'Forgive us our debts.' I have never so felt my need of the blood of Christ as after special times of blessing in preaching. Yet when we have freely stated all this, it does not mean that we are to continue in sin, if by sin be meant *known* evil. Christ came to save us from this. Christ came to heal us, not to leave His Church one general hospital of sick souls. We no

c

longer faithlessly say, ' I shall some day fall by the hand of the enemy,' but rather, 'I will yet praise Him more and more.'" Clearly this teaching was not sinlessness.

There were special gatherings of our foreign brethren, and Canon Christopher, *more suo*, gave a breakfast at the *Clarendon*, at which a large company gathered.

But the meeting that will live longest in memory is the " ministerial experience meeting " on the Wednesday evening ; certainly nothing like it ever came under the observation of the writer. It was proved to be unique from the fact that after its appointed hour ended, another announced meeting had to be given up, and the first continued. Later in the evening a sermon by the chairman, though on so longed-for a subject as " The Baptism of the Holy Ghost," had to be postponed for the same reason.

Ministers of all Churches were seated on and around the platform of the Corn Exchange ; the rest of the building was filled with other Christian people.

" The company ' had been with Jesus,' and something of childlike simplicity seemed to have been restored to their lives—a feeling which cannot be put into words, but which those at Oxford can never forget. The meeting opened with the ministers each giving his *present* experience of grace in a verse of Scripture : ' Christ who is our life ' ; ' No more I, but Christ ' ; ' My cup runneth over ' ; ' The Lord is risen indeed ' ; ' The Lord shall deliver me from every evil work ' ; ' Behold how good and how pleasant it is for brethren to dwell together in unity ' ; ' Now unto Him who is able to keep you from falling.' In a brief space a multitude of such testimonies of *present experience* were poured rapidly into our ears. We had heard witnesses for Jesus, but here was ' *a cloud* of witnesses.' The effect was marvellous. Never had the Scriptures seemed so full of present privilege. Could any one for a moment longer doubt the truths pressed upon our attention, or delay to grasp what seemed placed before us in letters of fire ? " The texts were followed by testimonies.

Pastor Stockmeyer : " Shall I give you the story of my past ? No ; it is buried. Yesterday I wrote to my wife that, by the almighty grace of the Lord, I am in fellowship with Him, and it is peace . . . I shall feel more and more a poor sinner, but I am impatient to finish with myself—I wish to be done with myself for ever . . . and I have the baptism of the Holy Ghost. *Theoretically I have known this blessing, but I have never fully realized it till now. There has been one thing in my heart not given up. By the grace of God I have cut the cable this afternoon.*"

Rev. E. W. Moore : " On May 1, '73, I was pressed to go and hear an address on this subject. I had disliked some papers on it, but I went. The speaker said that through heart searchings ' blessing had come to his life.' I said, ' Search *me*, O God,' and He did. A fortnight after I ventured, with bated breath, to say that it did seem as if the Lord Jesus had come and taken the throne of my heart. I can say to-day it is better than ever."

Rev. E. H. Hopkins : " This life makes Jesus so precious . . . no more worry. *God's will and my happiness are synonymous terms now.* The Lord has infinite things to teach, and ' it is better farther on.' "

Rev. Henry Sharpe : " I had preached against these views. At a prayer meeting here a dear friend stood up ; but I could not—my soul was in deep distress. On reaching our rooms the friend said, ' We must have the blessing together.' He prayed for me, and on rising asked, ' How is it now ? ' I said, ' The surrender is made.' But I had no joy that day. An experienced clergyman said, ' Thank God for what you have ; feeling will follow.' And it has. Never since my first forgiveness have I been so happy. Pray for me that I may make known to my people a full salvation."

Pasteur Monod : " We must come to the marriage supper of the Lamb, not bringing our own bit of bread, as we used to do at restaurants in the siege of Paris, but trusting Him to provide all. Some little thing, some foolish thing we are keeping, may stand in the way of blessing. This and all must be yielded. I gave myself to Christ without any feeling of faith, joy, or love, but still I did it, and after a time all these came to me."

There arose, with some trepidation, as one whom it cost a great deal to make confession, Canon Harford-Battersby, of whom his fellow-undergraduates in that Oxford had been wont to say years before, " There goes the man with the ten commandments in his face!" Notwithstanding such high-toned morality, and such earnest piety as marked his early years of ministry, he felt that there was something wanting. When the truths of sanctification by faith were proclaimed he hailed them as the very thing to supply that want. "I tried"—such are his words as given in the volume with which we have been refreshing our memory of this holy season—"I tried to say a word in defence of these doctrines, but I felt that I lacked the very blessing I advocated. Now, however, I have seen the simplicity of this way of faith and accepted it for myself. It is a difficult thing to speak of my own experience, and very distasteful; yet perhaps for this reason it may be right thus to acknowledge the blessing received."

Asked privately as to the time of its reception, Canon Battersby said to Mr. Hopkins : "Only last night, as you and Thornton were speaking about passing from seeking faith to resting faith, I passed over."

Besides these well-known names, quite a flood of speakers followed ; literally a flood, for it broke down all barriers. The stream of confession and testimony continued (if my memory serves me) from four o'clock till nine. What struck one most was the number of grave grey-headed men who spoke ; men, too, some of them naturally reticent, but who felt that this was not a time to keep silence, but a time to speak.

Another memorable meeting was that held on the Saturday morning in the Town Hall. Beautiful words had been spoken at the early prayer meeting : "Do not press this fulness of the Gospel on its dogmatic side. It is not so much a doctrine to be argued as a *life* to be lived. *Confess* CHRIST. Do not *profess* to be anything. Acknowledge His grace courageously, for nothing so reaches the hearts of others ; but remember that *you* are now no better in and of yourself—only you have learned that you may dare to trust Christ for more than you ever conceived of before. Your life must be your argument to those who see you constantly. Do not worry them by doctrinal statements, but love them into the fulness of salvation."

Lord Radstock, the Hon. Mr. Elout, and the Hon. T. W. Van Loome, from Amsterdam ; Pastor Appia, from Paris ; Pastor

Pank, from Berlin, gave brief bright words of testimony. And then, later in the morning, when Admiral Fishbourne bore to us greetings from Christians in Rome, it seemed as though we were all ready to join in Psalm ciii., on which the Rev. Filmer Sulivan commented ; or Psalm cxviii., the words of which, as they fell from Pasteur Monod's lips, with exultant joy, declared, " Blessed be the Lord who hath showed us light."

At a gathering before church time on Sunday morning the leader said : " You may have special temptations after this time of baptism. You may be tempted under the name of faith to do presumptuous things, or again to turn back to the world. Dread a cold life of mere duty, but *flee* fanaticism—the devil's lure for saintly souls. Never forget that the highest elevations of experience involve the greatest dangers. The sailor's safety at the mast head is in *looking up*. Be it ours to be ever 'looking unto Jesus.' "

Rev. F. Sulivan : " We have heard great things, and received great things. We have seen Jesus ! As we have gone on and on, there has been more and more unveiling of self, and then the Sun of Righteousness has risen with healing in His wings. May others take knowledge of us that we have been with Jesus—not with saints only—at Oxford ! ' All my springs are in *Thee* '—not in the Oxford Conference, but in Jesus."

At the evening meeting the chairman said : " Have you any wedge of gold, any Babylonish garment left ? Bring them to the valley of Achor, burn them with fire, raise over them a heap of stones, so that you shall never see them again. At Waterloo the possession of a little cottage decided the fate of nations. So Satan entrenches himself in some small thing in the will ; hundreds have said in this room that it was, in yielding their last reserve, they found full Communion. Bring that reserve to Achor. He will give you your ' vineyards,' your joy, ' from thence ' ; thou shall call Him ' Husband,' and no more call Him ' Master,' and He will betroth thee unto Him for ever (Hosea ii. 14–21). Scripture opens with an earthly marriage and closes with a heavenly, and throughout its pages are types and songs for those, themselves risen, who are ' married to Him who is raised from the dead.' May we never let our hearts go out again to any conflicting love. *The Lord save us from preaching high doctrine and living low practice!"*

Next day the Rev. J. Turner (Vicar of Deddington) gave this testimony : " The difficulties in my parish were so great that I felt like a lion in a cage, and prayed to be removed to some other place of work. Thank God, I have learned during these happy days—the happiest of my life—to be content ' in that state of life unto which' God called me. Yesterday morning I gave notice that at the evening service I would tell of the outpouring of the Spirit at these Oxford meetings. The church was crowded, one Nonconformist closing his place, another shortening his service, and each bringing his people to join us. At an after meeting, at which I was helped by Mr. Richardson, of St. Benet's, London, there was such a scene as we had never had in the memory of living men, though we have had many seasons of blessing. Some gave themselves to Christ for the first time, and others experienced a fresh baptism of the Spirit."

At the same Monday morning's meeting, Mr. Varley said : " Paul began with, ' What wilt Thou have me to *do* ? ' but ended with, ' I have kept the faith.' Oh, sirs, it was faith that subdued kingdoms, obtained promises ! Put your foot on each promise and say, ' It is mine.' "

The Rev. Baron Hart, of Paris, said : " The meetings have been a real blessing to me—not in any great joy or rapture, but in finding full rest in the Lord. A wonderful change since those dark times when I had to teach to others what I did not fully receive myself."

At one of the ladies' meetings attention was called to Psalm cxviii. 8. " It is better to trust in the Lord than to put confidence in man." While bowed before the Lord they sang with deep feeling—

> " I am trusting, Lord, in Thee,
> Dear Lamb of Calvary ;
> Humbly at Thy Cross I bow,
> Jesus saves me—saves me now."

From one and another burden after burden was rolled off weary shoulders and laid on Jesus. One lady said : " Lord, I trust Thee with my dissipated son." Another said : " Lord,

I trust Thee with my Bible-women." Another—"Lord, I trust Thee with my business." Another—"Lord, I trust Thee with my health." It was a deeply impressive time.

After rising from our knees a lady rose and said that she had attended many a *prayer* meeting before, but never a *trust* meeting."

At another of the ladies' meetings a letter was read from Miss Havergal, from Switzerland, where she and her friends, following a guide who cut steps for them in the snow, found themselves continually stumbling. At last one of the party called out to the rest, " If you will put your feet *exactly* in the steps of the guide, you will find it quite easy to walk." They tried, and found it true ; so it was shown that implicit following the Lord, with perfect confidence in His power and wisdom to guide, would make an easy path through the most difficult places.

An eminent worker for Christ rose and said : " I have been a Christian for thirty years, and a rejoicing one too, but I had not perfect inward victory, nor perfect rest. My daughter received this teaching joyfully, and has lived in the power of it for more than a year. I prayed and struggled and read. The day before I came here I asked the Lord to show me what was the matter. Suddenly, as though scales had fallen from my eyes, I saw it. All these years I had been holding on to Christ, and my weak grasp had often seemed almost to fail with the strain. Now I saw that Christ was holding me, and instead of straining, I might fall back and rest in His strong and loving embrace."

Another earnest Christian worker said : " I know something of the life of faith, but I want to know the life of union also. We must put our wills—the mainspring of our beings—into His hands, and then simply trust Him to work in us mightily. Then we shall thirst for souls, have power to overcome, be gentle, meek, and easy to be entreated. We shall, in short, be Christlike. Dear friends, it is the only way ; let us get life within, and it will be manifested outwardly."

A lady well known for her life-long faithfulness prayed : " Oh, Lord ! Thou hast been walking through Oxford with royal progress. Those who have come here longing for the life in God, have entered upon it. Those who knew something of it before, have found a nearer communion. We are waiting on Thee for further revelations of Thine unutterable beauty and strength. Let the sweetness of Thy love be a perpetual power over every thought, look and action. Take us out of self, and self out of us. Let us each go home with such a presence of Thee around us, that others shall see, not only that we have been with Jesus, but that Jesus has come back with us."

Surely our sisters had blessings as rich as any in the general meetings. Their "creeds and doctrines," writes the memorialist, "were not changed, but their experience was. They laid hold of the things which, hitherto, they had, too much, only talked about. They dropped the future tense out of God's blessings, which had heretofore put them off indefinitely, and adopted the tense of present realization. It was no longer, ' I trust He *will* do,' but, ' I know He *has* done.' "

There were several side-meetings held in Oxford, some of them quite private, and there were also meetings very specially public—meetings in the Market Place. Was it at one of these that a countryman was heard to give his idea of the Convention in the words : " It's all the Christian folk in all the world going to be one sect " ?

Lord Radstock was foremost in these open-air meetings, and rising at a Convention gathering, he appealed for helpers, and not a few went forth to aid in the effort to evangelize. We shall not know until the great day the effect of their efforts.

" A dear child of seventeen, said to me," we read in this review, " I cannot tell you anything about the grand buildings at Oxford, but I know a good deal about the small lanes. We went there with some ministers singing for Jesus, and the people followed us in troops, and dear J. W. preached the Gospel to them ; and now I am longing to go back to school to tell them all about the blessing."

" And if it be asked what is the ' blessing ? ' it is the blessedness of the man ' who maketh the Lord his trust '; ' whose strength is in Thee '; of them who have not seen and yet have believed ; who stand by night in the house of the Lord, trusting where they cannot see Him ; who present their bodies a living sacrifice, holy, acceptable to God, their reasonable service ; and who, doing this, are not conformed to this world, but are being daily ' transformed by the renewing of their

minds, that ' they ' may know what is that good and acceptable
and perfect will of the Lord.' "

It were vain to try to tell the effects of that wonderful Conference. They are found to this day in many a corner of
England, and in many another Conference in this and other
lands ; better still, they are found in many holy, useful, happy
lives. One immediate effect was in gifts which poured in, one
of them an anonymous cheque for £1,000. This was used for
Continental work. That work was still more forwarded by
the press. The *Faith Hymns* [1] were translated into German
and French, as also were books on the life of faith. In Paris
the monthly periodical *La Libérateur*, and in Basle *Des Chris-
ten Glaubensweg*, were at once commenced, and devoted specially, like *The Christian's Pathway of Power* in England, to
teaching the privileges of a life of trust. So, as in Wycliffe's
time, as in Wesley's, Oxford became a centre from which there
sounded out the word of the Lord unto vast regions beyond.

---

[1] These were accompanied, and some of them set to music by the Rev.
James Mountain. Dr. Mountain is a welcome visitor at Keswick to
this day. He and Rev. T. Ryder (who died soon after) rendered
most valuable help at Oxford, Brighton, and in many places. Few
living men were so conversant with the inner circle of the Movement
in its early days.

CHAPTER IV

THE MORNING GLORY

THE BRIGHTON CONVENTION

" Strangers from a distant land,
Led by Jesu's loving hand,
We have met upon this shore,
Strangers, foreigners no more.
Jesus was our meeting-place
As we sought our Father's face ;
One word made all hearts to glow :
' Jesus saves me, saves me now.'

" Broken, broken at His feet,
Thus for His blest use made meet :
Emptied of all things below,
Him and only Him to know ;
Helpless, worthless, weak and poor,
He our strength, our boundless store ;
Nothing we, nor great, nor small,
Jesus Christ, our All in All."

HISTORIANS of religious movements when recording events of 1875 will surely take account of the Mission taken by the prince of evangelists, Mr. Moody, in the London Opera House, and of the Convention held, under the leadership of another American, in the Brighton Dome.

On the first day of this Convention a message was read from Mr. Moody from that day's meeting in Covent Garden, in which he said, " Let us lift up our hearts to seek earnestly a blessing on the great Convention that is now being held in Brighton, perhaps the most important meeting ever gathered." And Mr. Pearsall Smith, the Brighton chairman, said, " Let us ask an answering blessing upon our beloved brother, Mr. Moody, a man who walks with God."

It is difficult to realize that the meetings at Oxford and

34

Brighton, and the first Convention at Keswick, were all held within a twelvemonth. But so it was, and they are united by golden cords.

It was at Oxford that Canon Battersby stepped into the rest of faith. It was at Brighton that he announced the intention of holding meetings at Keswick. At this period multitudes of Christians were lamenting their constant slavery to some indurated habit of sin—if indeed they got so far as to lament it. But the word had gone forth that "God had visited His people." "I know but one sentence in German," said he, "whose trumpet-tones had just stirred the land of Luther, 'Jesus errettet mich jetzt' ['Jesus saves me now']; but this is enough to carry me safe through life and up into glory." The words were a line of a hymn which was then being sung by thousands abroad. Another hymn, written in English, though not by an Englishman, conveyed to thousands of our countrymen the thoughts of the new land of promise which prophetic eyes were opened to see. We mean Monod's hymn, "Oh! the bitter pain and sorrow."

So hope began to spread her wings, and not a few, eager to soar with her, listened to the invitation to meet God at Brighton with ardour and with expectation.

One estimate of the numbers brings them up to seven thousand, and doubtless, at least, that number came to the town for the Convention in the course of the week. The most manifest test of the extent of the gathering was that the Dome and Corn Exchange, each holding between two and three thousand people, were daily both of them filled morning, afternoon, and evening; the old Town Hall, which held nearly another thousand, and the rooms in the Pavilion, holding between them another thousand more, might all be simultaneously filled also. The number of nationalities represented was remarkable, the hearts of very many French and Swiss Protestants were stirred by the accounts their pastors had given them of what they had learnt at Oxford; and the hearts of German, Dutch and Italian Christians by visits of Mr. Pearsall Smith, the Chairman of both Conventions.

When those from foreign lands were asked to rise, there stood up under the Dome some seventy Christian leaders, "twenty-three nationalities being represented." Nor can we forget that it was a French pastor who swayed the great gathering night by night, a Swiss College Principal who presided at one of the Communion services, and a German at another. Nor was anything more touching than that, so soon after the Franco-German War, Christians from both those countries fraternized and forgot their controversies in Christ. On the two Sunday evenings of the Convention Pastor Monod, from Paris, and Dr. Prochnow, from Berlin, occupied the same pulpit (that of what was then the writer's church) in succession. In that church on that first Sunday morning in June the communicants filled not only the floor, but the galleries of the church. A memorable address was given to them by Mr. Stevenson—afterwards Sir Arthur—Blackwood. He spoke there another day that week, in words which were recalled years after as having been the turning-point in the life of a gentleman casually visiting Brighton.

But let us return to the Convention proper, and try to give something like an idea of the feast of fat things spread before us.

It began with a Praise Meeting in the Dome on Saturday, May 29, 1875, at 7 a.m. There was a similar meeting for each of the ten days. "A gathering of 3,000 at seven in the morning was itself an imposing scene. Our friend who had the leadership of the meetings seemed at these times to be specially endued with the power of the Holy Spirit, and opened out the deepest Scriptural truths, and led our devotions into the very sanctuary of the Divine Presence. In true harmony with these exercises was the deeply impressive manner in which the requests for prayer were presented at these times ; also the devotional singing of such hymns as ' I need Thee every hour,' ' Only Thee, my soul's Redeemer,' ' Not a sound invades the stillness,' etc."

Referring to 2 Chronicles xx., which he had read, and to the fact that we began with a praise meeting, the Chairman told how, when Louis XIII was with Mazarin before a city of the Huguenots, the whole multitude of the besieged, though nearly at the point of starvation, came out upon the walls and sang one of their wonderful hymns of praise. The king said to his minister : " We can do nothing with such a people ! " and he beat a retreat. " So Satan would do before the people Israel when they praised God with a loud voice. So, if when any

temptation comes you will say aloud, or in a whisper, ' Praise
the Lord ' ; if overwhelmed with care, ' Praise the Lord ' ;
if in an agony of sorrow (for the life of faith does not make us
stoics), ' Praise the Lord,' it will take the power out of the
temptation, the pressure off the care, and the sting and restlessness out of the agony."

The Rev. Evan Hopkins appropriately chose for the same
meeting Psalm ciii., urging that praise " should be the exercise
of the *whole man*—' all that is within me.'   See that we count
up God's mercies, instead of dwelling on our miseries.   And
' great are ' His ' mercies,' ' who forgiveth, healeth, redeemeth,
crowneth, satisfieth.'   How true of the man who trusts with
his whole heart ! "

After prayer and singing, the brethren from the Continent
were specially referred to, and about seventy rose to receive
our welcome.   " While these stood, the congregation joined
in earnest prayer for blessing on them " during their stay in
England and on their return to their own lands.   And in clear
but slow tones Herr Lippert, of Frankfort, expressed the
feeling of his brethren when he said :   " Our hearts from the
Continent have come over to England, and American hearts
have even crossed the ocean, to join the dear English hearts
with whom we now feel so happily one."   The meeting closed
with the hymn, " Jesus erretet mich jetzt," sung by its author,
Pasteur Gebhart, from Zürich.

Time would fail to tell of the meetings that followed quick
and fast that day and the other days of the succeeding week.
The volume of interest deepened as it rolled on, and the enthusiasm swelled into a mighty tide, the like of which one has
rarely, if ever, seen.   Such was the enthusiasm that each
afternoon people crowded together to listen to Bible-readings
by Mrs. Pearsall Smith, with interest so keen that the Great
Dome could not hold the numbers that came ; and after the
earliest days the readings had to be repeated an hour later in the
Corn Exchange.   M. Monod's addresses were also specially blest.

Shall we try to give our readers an idea of an address or two
by each of these speakers ?

Mrs. Pearsall Smith, taking the subject of the overcoming
life, said : " I will not call it the higher Christian life, but simply
the life of the believer.   Here is a little pyramid of texts about

it : John x. 10 ; Ephesians ii. 1–10 ; Colossians iii. 1–3 ; 1
John iii. 24, etc. It is a resurrection life, as if one had died
and been buried, and risen again. How do people get delivered
from the foolishness of childhood ? Not by being scolded out of
it, or by making efforts to get out of it, but by growing out
of it. Again we are told that ' if we walk in the Spirit we
are not under the law.' That does not mean that the right
things are not done, but that they are done from the force of
an inward love, not from the constraint of an outward law.
I knew a lady who was a Christian, but a . very uncomfortable and unhappy Christian, and made everybody unhappy
around her. She kept good enough in her own room, but
when with the family all her prickles came out. She was
pointed to Romans vi. and urged to read it verse by verse on
her knees. ' Ask the Lord to show you what it means and
believe it, and you will get deliverance.' She read till she
came to verse 11, ' Reckon yourselves to be dead unto sin.'
' I am not dead,' she said, ' it would be telling a story, if I said
that.' At last she made up her mind to obey the command,
and on the authority of God's Word to reckon herself dead to
sin. She claimed it by faith over and over ; she went to sleep
doing it ; she got up in the morning doing it ; she did it as she
went downstairs ; she went through breakfast saying it to
herself, and the Lord made it true. ' Has anything happened,'
said her mother to her, ' you seem to be so happy ? ' She
replied that it seemed to her as if her soul had sailed into
Heaven. Since then, for three years, she had been living the
overcoming life, reckoning herself dead to sin in Christ Jesus."

The addresses of Pasteur Theodore Monod evening after
evening were full of power, and grace, and blessing. Let us
listen to him as he takes us with Moses in the desert to the
burning bush. When Moses saw the bush he thought the fire
would go out and leave nothing but ashes ; but it went on burning, burning, and Moses said : ' I will now turn aside and see
. . . and when the Lord saw that he turned aside, God called
him by name.' And Moses did not say, ' I want to know how
that Voice speaks my name.' He answered at once : ' Here am
I.' And we might spend a lifetime and more in trying to
understand the great mystery of God's existence and of God's
revealing Himself. There is something better to do. It is to

answer straightway : ' Here am I.'   Then He will make us feel
that He has ' come down to deliver us out of the hand of the
Egyptians.'

" God wants to be to each of us the very fire that was in
the bush, the fire which is its own fuel, which feeds upon itself
and never burns out—the life of God.   You ask what will
feed the life of God in you ?   Why God Himself ; God is the
life of God.   You need not bring your sticks of wood to keep
up that fire.   The bush burned and was not consumed.   Let it
burn you up ; let it burn up your selfishness, burn the evil
passions out of you, cause you to suffer, but also to rejoice.   It
is a burning fire, a consuming fire, a purifying fire, a fire of
love, a fire of joy.   The fire that Christ came to kindle in this
world, the fire of which it was said ' He will baptize you
with the Holy Ghost and with fire.' "

On the fifth day, M. Monod told of a beautiful house shown
him when returning from the Oxford Convention, whose owner,
the richest man in the place, believed himself to be the poorest,
and used to break stones by the road.   " Of course, he was
out of his mind.   So are a good many people now, spiritually."

I dare not quote many of these memorable addresses, but
it were criminal to omit the one on Peter walking on the water.
" Before he could do that he had to come down out of the ship—
this miserable ship, this crazy old ship, you say, and so on.   But
when it comes to getting out of it, that is the trying moment.
Peter slipped over the side of the vessel, but still held on with
one hand.   Then came the secret command : ' Peter, unloose
your fingers ; let go the boat.'   That is God's word to you—
let go the boat (the boat's name is Self).   ' Ah,' you say,
' this is dreadful.'   It is not dreadful ; it is the greatest blessing.   ' Let go the boat ! Oh !' you say, ' and go like a
stone to the bottom ? '   No, Peter got out of the ship, ' and
walked *on* the water.'   Instead of swallowing him up, it bore
him up.   And why did he ' walk on the water ' ?   ' To go to
Jesus.'   And to go to Jesus he had to look to Jesus.   There
was no path marked out before him ; his path was just a straight
line from where he was to where Jesus was—all the path that
we shall ever have.   He moved right on for a little.   The wind,
however, kept on blowing, and seemed worse than ever.   So
' Peter began to be afraid,' and as soon as he began to be

afraid he began to sink. He did not quite trust the Lord's power. He thought, now this is really wonderful, but how long will it last? When a man begins to ask that, it's not likely to last very long. He thought of wind and waves, not of the Lord, and began to sink. Then he cried out : ' Lord, save me.' A very good prayer, but there is something better, viz., to walk calmly on, trusting in the Lord. Jesus did not answer, ' How very humble and pious of you to cry, Lord, save me ! ' He said, ' Oh, thou of little faith, wherefore didst thou doubt ? ' Let me assure you, the Christian life does not consist in crying continually, ' Lord, save me.' By all means let us so cry, when we *do* begin to sink, and when He has set us on our feet again, let us go on trusting. But if it is glory to Him to rescue us when we sink, it is greater glory to keep us from sinking."

A solemn stillness fell upon the meeting, which lasted several minutes. It was closed by the following words, repeated by many voices : " I know whom I have believed, and am persuaded that He is able to keep that which I have committed unto Him against that day."

Our limits shut out addresses by many teachers, and a host of testimonies—some from far India and Australia. Some of the speakers were not heard again on these platforms, as Mr. and Mrs. Smith, Dr. Asa Mahan, Admiral Fishbourne, Mr. Haig Miller, and many from the Continent of Europe. Others are happily with us to this day, the Revs. W. H. Webb-Peploe, E. H. Hopkins, and E. W. Moore. Mr. Varley, who spoke with great power, had been testifying almost to the day in the spring of 1912, when in this very Brighton he went home to God.

We must quote a word of witness spoken by Preb. Webb Peploe—" There was a watching, waiting and struggling to do right, yet I constantly found myself overcome and generally unable to realize anything like St. Paul's experience, ' Not I, but Christ liveth in me.' Was his an ideal picture, I asked, or is it possible for me to realize it ? After a time, I saw that if I believed it would be mine. When we believe that what God Almighty says will be fulfilled in our hearts, the soul drops into the hands of the Lord Jesus, for Him to use for His own glory. I know that there are many cares which bring the minister low, and which in former days made it seem to me impossible to obey the calls to service. But when the truth came—'Not I, but Christ that liveth in me'—the rest of faith was practically known in my ministerial life."

Again and again a meeting was held for ministers, and one or two testimonies may be culled from the many recorded. The chairman told of a teamster brought to the Lord—a fighting, swearing man. When he went down to work, a man purposely rolled a heavy box on his feet and hurt him much. In his old days he would have knocked the man down ; now he said to himself, ' The blood cleanseth,' and freely forgave. Another time he was insulted, he merely repeated ' the blood cleanseth.' "

Pastor Streetz, from Silesia : " I read of a meeting to be held in Berlin. I went there as an earthly pilgrim, but returned as a citizen of the Heavenly Jerusalem. God's Word was illuminated ; sins which used to beset me I could put aside ; a stream of peace came into my heart, and it has not been lost in the sands of the desert."

Dr. Prochnow : " The devil often troubles Christians by temptations at which they are horrified, and then tries to make them accuse themselves of having sinned."

Pastor Reichenbach, of Basle : " I was invited last year to Oxford, but did not go, as I felt that I must be alone with God to receive the light I needed. I studied the Bible and, to my unspeakable joy, I saw that, as my sins had been washed away, so the power of my sins had been crucified with Christ, and I could consider the evil in my heart—and Satan too—as overcome by One who is mightier. If we are in Christ we belong to Him Who is THE MASTER OF THE WORLD."

Mr. Backhouse, of Sunderland, said : " When young, I served myself, not God. I went on sinning and repenting. However, I was led to see that I must look to Christ alone for help ; I did so and obtained it. Though I have had failures, yet the Lord has kept me until now ; and I desire that all I have should be the Lord's."

Pastor Schrenk, of the Basle Mission, said : " I offered myself for missionary work and was accepted, but I saw that my spiritual life did not agree with the promises of Scripture. There was an immense gulf between them. For six months I

D

was in this state. One evening the words came to me, ' They
have washed their robes and made them white in the blood of
the Lamb ; *therefore* are they before the throne of God.'
I thought, if those before the throne have nothing but the blood
of Christ, it would be sufficient for me. From that moment I
had the peace of God in my heart."

Mr. Haig Miller : " It was the property of the former spiritual life to hold its flavour for two or three days, after we
had inhaled some of the fragrance of the everlasting hills ; but
now I trust Jesus to help me as soon as I wake and would pray,
and He does in that ; when I come down to breakfast—in the
simple matter of eating—and He does in that ; when I go
to the city, in the cares (hardly cares now) of business, and He
does in that. And—I say it humbly—my wife would tell you,
she has got a new husband, my servants that they have
found a new master, and my employees that the little foxes
that spoiled the vines are now killed."

There were meetings for inquiry—indeed, the only meeting
in which the writer took any part was one of these, in which
he shared the responsibilities with Mr. Bowker. These meetings
were helpful in dealing with difficulties scriptural and practical.

Then there were many meetings for foreign pastors.

One was a breakfast meeting at Mellison's Hall, at which
the Earl of Kintore presided. About one hundred and sixty
pastors accepted the invitation. Representatives from each
country were asked to say grace, and the words of thanksgiving fell in German, French, Austrian, Belgian, Dutch, Swiss,
Italian, Swedish, Norwegian, Spanish,—from those living in
China and America, from an Indian missionary in some Hindoo
dialect, and from Bishop Gobat (as coming from Jerusalem)
in Hebrew. A similar gathering (in each there were some
English friends) was held at Stanmer Park, the seat of the
revered Earl of Chichester, who, however, was compelled to
be away at a meeting of the Ecclesiastical Commission. In
his absence the large company was received by his son, the
Hon. Thomas Pelham, who had been taking part in the evangelistic services at Brighton. Madame Rappard, daughter
of Bishop Gobat, of Jerusalem, composed a farewell hymn,
of which two verses are given at the head of this chapter, and
one more must be added here—

" English brethren ! Fare ye well,
God's rich blessings on you dwell !
We would clasp your hands and say,
Ere we tear ourselves away,
' Oh ! let this our watchword be,
Jesus saveth even me.'
Let us trust, whate'er befall,
Let us trust Him—that is all."

The climax of the Convention was appropriately reached
in the United Communion Service. On the previous Sunday
multitudes gathered round the Lord's table in various churches.
One has been referred to already. Another, that at St. Margaret's (where the Rev. Filmer Sulivan was then Incumbent),
was, says the Report, made very special. Close to in " the
Eglise Réformée Française," a German and French pastor
administered the service of love to nearly two hundred Continental brethren."

But all this was felt to be insufficient to give vent to the tide
of Christian longing. This could only find fitting expression in
a common Communion Service. As the writer happened to
pass through the committee room when the question was under
discussion, Admiral Fishbourne asked whether he thought the
Dome or Corn Exchange the more suitable place. " I wonder,"
was the reply, " whether both halls may not be needed." Both
accordingly were set apart and both were filled, so that nearly
five thousand communicants must have participated at that
weekday service of the Holy Supper.

At the same hour some hundred members of the Society of
Friends assembled in their wonted place of worship, to feast
with their Lord in their own spiritual manner. " Some
' Friends,' however, participated in the general service ; and
more would have done so, but for seeming separation from
their own brethren."

This gathering was not only unique in numbers but in the
choice of ministrants. In the Dome Dr. Prochnow, of Berlin,
presided. He held both Lutheran and Anglican Orders,
having received the latter as a C.M.S. Missionary in the Himalayas : but he had returned to work in Berlin. He was
assisted by several foreign pastors from the twenty-three
nationalities represented amongst us.

In the Corn Exchange M. Rappard, of Chrischrona, presided, M. Monod, Mr. Smith, and other leaders of the Convention sitting silent by.
Zinzendorf's hymn,

"I thirst, Thou wounded Lamb of God."

was sung ; several pastors then read verses of Scripture, texts from the Apocalypse, like that in chapter i 5, which speaks of the " love " and the " blood ; " that in v. 8, which speaks of " the Lamb " and " the blood-washed " with " the harps, the vials, and the odours," striking the key-notes of union among Christians, through communion with Christ.

After reading the fifty-first Psalm, the congregation rose and repeated Isaiah's sentence, " All we like sheep have gone astray, we have turned every one to his own way, and the Lord hath laid on Him the iniquity of us all ; " which Prof. Rappard followed with such assurances of God's pardon as " Thy sins are forgiven thee," " I have blotted out as a cloud thy transgressions, and as a thick cloud thy sins ; return unto Me, for I have redeemed thee."

The only Englishman who took audible part in either Communion Service, and he hailed from afar, was Mr. Lawrence of Barcelona—for it was arranged, at once to bring different nations into one, and to avoid questions of differing churches at home, that the foreign pastors should administer the sacred elements to their English brethren.

In the Dome the combined hymn,

" Jesus Lover of my soul,
" Rock of Ages, cleft for me,"

was repeatedly sung, the place of singing being taken in the other assembly by the continued utterance of sweetly-culled passages of Scripture, so that many voices were heard ; but the words were the words of God—words like these : " Who His own self bore our sins in His own body on the tree ; " " I am the Good Shepherd ; " " the Good Shepherd giveth His life for the sheep ; " " I am come that they might have life, and that they might have it more abundantly." Indeed, the intensely scriptural character of the whole service was the most striking thing about it. This great service of praise, a true eucharistia, was followed by thanksgiving meetings the next morning. The Corn Exchange being crammed, some, as on other mornings, gathered in the Dome, where Pasteur Monod said—" I suppose you, like myself, are disappointed. Let us remember, however, that our *dis*appointments are God's *appointments*. It is not enough to say that we must ' make the best of it ' ; we must believe that it *is* the best. I will leave with you, as a memento, two very short words. The first is ' Thou ! ' The word that comes most naturally to us is the word ' I.' ' I am wise, I am deserving, I have need of nothing.' By-and-by, we learn by grace to say, ' I am poor, I am guilty, I am helpless.' Then we go on to say, ' Not I, but Christ,' ' I am saved by *Him*, rich in Him.' A great step, but there is another. It is good to speak *of* Christ, it is better to speak *to* Christ. So let our hearts go out to our Saviour, for ' To look to our experience for comfort is to warm ourselves in the moonlight,' as Pasteur Bost said. ' So THOU art the truth, the life, the love ; I need *Thee*, I have *Thee*, O Lord Jesus ! '

And when do we have Him ? *Now*. Now is God's time. Past joys, past sorrows, past sins, past grace ; leave them in the past, and trust in the Lord *now*. As to the morrow, He expressly bids us take no thought for it. Besides, what do we know about the future ?

Now, therefore, the only moment in which we have, or ever will have, to live, let us keep saying, not to ourselves, but to our God and Saviour,

' THOU ! '
' NOW ! ' "

A Pastor from Holland said—" I came here as a looker-on strongly *prejudiced*. I thought the movement was not orthodox, even now I am not sure that the doctrine is quite straight. But this I know, there is a good thing to be had, a blessing which thousands have received, and I have got it. It came to me chiefly through hearing the words. ' Won't you trust Jesus ? ' —words I had myself spoken to others many a time. Now I have given myself to Him altogether and am happy in Him."

Pastor Comba, from Italy—" I can testify to having received a great blessing here. I was converted to God before, after having been an unbeliever. I have learned here that working and talking for God is not everything. I had been so busy that

Jesus Christ had not time to talk to me—just as visitors sometimes do, never giving one a chance to put a word in. Now,
here at Brighton, I have found, not a new Jesus, but the same
Jesus I had known before, saying to me, ' Will you kindly
stop and let Me talk to you ? ' And the Lord has talked to me.
I have obtained not so much impressions as a new direction to
my life."

Pastor Riggenbach, of Basle : " My first word on awaking
this morning was, ' I am so glad ! ' And why so glad ? Because Jesus loves me. I have many burdens, but I lay them
on Him ; *many burdens but no cares."*

Pastor Diestelkamp, of Berlin. " There is a celebrated and
well-known window in the King's palace, where he frequently
stands while speaking to his Ministers. This window looks out
upon the thoroughfare. One day the King did not at once
answer the Minister of State when he entered the room ;
and why ? Because he was smiling upon a poor man in the
street, who was lifting up his little boy in his arms, as high as
he could, that the child might get a good look at the King.
Just so, our dear English brethren have lifted us up in their
arms, that we should get a nearer sight of the dear, holy face
of our heavenly Father."

In the Corn Exchange Mr. Varley said : " We share
Heaven's joy, ' It was good that we should make *merry.'*
What a word ! No mere man could have written it. Last
night, after the preaching of Christ at the Town Hall, fifty-one
professed to accept Him. Amongst them were five old men.
There was one, an aged man, about seventy, an advocate, who
came up and grasped my hand, almost pulling me off the platform in his grateful joy ; and whilst we rejoiced together,
two young women pressed through the crowd, and threw themselves weeping on the old man's neck. They were his daughters, rejoicing also in their newly-found Saviour. I could only
take the old man in my arms and weep with him. And this
morning, when many were already in tears, a loud voice,
broken with emotion, cried from one side of the room, ' Oh,
it is true, it is true ; I am the man ! ' and for a few moments
only the voice of weeping could be heard throughout the great
assembly. The burst of thanksgiving found relief in singing
together the chorus.

' Hallelujah Thine the Glory.' "

Among his closing words, as he held up his Bible, were
these,—" I pray God to keep every one of us within the covers
of His Book."

After other words and a hymn,

Mr. Pearsall Smith continued : " We should now like to
commend our brethren from abroad in special prayer to God,
if they will rise. Will our friends from India rise ? "

In silence, one here and another there, all over the room,
rose, as each succeeding nationality was mentioned :

" And those from China,
And from Australia,
And from America,
And from Jerusalem,
And from Africa,
And from the Sandwich Islands,
And from France,
And from Germany,
And from Switzerland,
And from Holland,
And from Belgium,
And from Norway,
And from Sweden,
And from Russia,
And from Austria,
And from Italy,
And from Spain,
And from Persia,

And any others who are not dwellers in Great Britain or
Ireland."

" Glory, honour, praise and power,"

was sung, and special prayer offered for the Queen, the Prince
of Wales, and the Royal Family.

After a spontaneous committing of each other to God, the
Rev. W. Hay Chapman pronounced the Benediction, and the
Chairman said :

" The Brighton Convention has now ended, and the blessings from the Convention have begun."

CHAPTER V

"TO YOUR TENTS, O ISRAEL."

"Magnificent
The morning rose, in memorable pomp,
Glorious as e'er I had beheld—in front
The sea lay laughing at a distance; near
The solid mountains shone, bright as the clouds, drenched in empyrean
    light;
And in the meadows and the lower grounds
Was all the sweetness of a common dawn—
Dews, vapours, and the melody of birds,
And labourers going forth to till the fields.
Ah! need I say, dear friend, that to the brim
My heart was full, I made no vows, but vows
Were then made for me; bond unknown to me
Was given, that I should be, else sinning greatly,
A dedicated spirit."

WORDSWORTH.

ROMANISM has its Retreats, New England has its North-field. Is Protestantism to have no Retreat and *Old* England no Camp Meeting or similar gathering? The answer to both questions, God's answer, as we believe, is the Keswick Convention.

The very scene of it is most alluring. Is there a lovelier landscape in England than that which looks out on fair Derwentwater, surrounded by its rampart of hills, while at their feet lies the lake with its creeks, bays and islands? The lower hills—and the higher to their shoulders—are clothed with a wealth of verdure rarely equalled and never surpassed. Although we miss the *arbutus* of Kerry, yet even an Irishman finds it difficult to contend for the superiority of Killarney. The Scotchman is more *dour*, and we heard of a Highland visitor to Derwentwater whose best praise was given in the words "Just like Heaven! Just like Scotland!"

This was the spot which " the tender mercy of our God" chose to be the scene of the manifestation of the gifts of His Spirit on a scale rarely known elsewhere in these islands for a generation. We do not wonder, for the God of nature and the God of grace are one ; and we hold it to be a distinct advantage that those who " worship the Lord in the beauty of holiness," should find themselves convened in a spot, where also physically " the beauty of the Lord our God is upon us." That in the intervals of united worship, the voice of praise and the ripple of the oar should be heard in unison is no drawback. And that the lessons learnt in the Tents should be thought over in Borrowdale, and on the heights of Skiddaw is all to the good. Yes, nature has helped grace in the call to Keswick ; and impressions of the teaching have been deepened in the scenes where " there is no speech nor language," save that of " the still small Voice."

There are other striking associations of the place. Who can forget " The Lake poets " the greatest of them, the greatest of all English poets of nature, William Wordsworth, lived across the hills at Rydal, and now sleeps hard by. There is no group of graves in England more appropriately placed than those of the poet and his kindred in Grasmere Churchyard. Within a motor ride, at Coniston, lies all that is left of John Ruskin, a great poet too in his way. While at Keswick itself, in Crosthwaite Church, is the tomb of Southey, the Laureate, who by his prose, more than by his poetry. by such books as the *Life of Wesley,* for instance, took an abiding place in English literature.

It was our joy to be lodged in a house in the grounds of what was Southey's residence during a recent Convention, and in earlier years to be welcomed to the adjacent house. There for a brief spell Coleridge lived. Archdeacon Hare speaks of him as " the Christian philosopher, who, through dark and winding paths of speculation was led to the light, in order that others by his guidance might reach that light, without passing through the darkness." The volume to which this is the dedication is " *The Mission of the Comforter.*" Little did the gifted author think that that *Mission* would receive its most marked acknowledgment for the end of the nineteenth and beginning of the twentieth centuries, just on the spot where that " great Christian philosopher " fought his hardest battle. The Churches of Keswick have held a notable position in sympathy with such notable memories. The name of Canon Rawnsley is honourably known by his sonnets, by his promotion of the industries of Keswick, and his plea for the preservation of the sanctity of its scenery.

In St. John's Church there ministered for a generation one who was in the van of enquirers after truth—the author of *Catholic Thoughts*, the Rev. Frederic Myers. In his advancing years. he was looking for a curate. A young clergyman in the South, hearing of the need, journeyed all the way to Keswick to see one who had become his literary and religious hero. This was the Rev. T. D. Harford-Battersby. He was a Balliol man : amongst his contemporaries at Oxford were Matthew Arnold, Lord Coleridge and Archbishop Temple. He had been for awhile lured into worldly ways. Then, he was caught in Newman's net—the great preacher at this time preaching his arresting sermons in Oxford. Under his spell Battersby became curate to one who held Tractarian views. But his conscience pricked him, his father and his uncle, (Mr. Harford, of Blaise Castle,) warned him, and at last " the snare was broken, and his soul escaped." Just then Mr. Myers' book [1] fell into his hands, and he exchanged Gosport for Keswick, and High-Churchism for Broad-Churchism. The one however scarcely satisfied him more than the other, and it was not long before he, who had " feared to be thought an Evangelical," swung back, heart and soul, into its full Scriptural position. Not that he ever became narrow. He speedily gathered into united effort people of all churches, and, after he had become Mr. Myers' successor, his light and love told more and more upon all the people of the town. For he most keenly felt as if he had been " merely playing with things hitherto, while souls have to be won for Christ by earnest wrestling and unsparing pains." Still he described himself as " an unhappy creature in the 7th of Romans." As late as February, 1856 we find him asking " What victory has been

---

[1] On May 15, 1849, Canon Battersby makes this entry in his diary : " Read Myers on *Church and Ministry*. I seem to find a guide and a prophet in him."

gained ? What evil habit overcome ? One thing I have begun
to understand, to look out of myself more. I praise God for
this ! But I scarcely dare congratulate myself upon it ;
there is so much to be done ; my enemies are legion." And,
in 1873,—" I feel that I am dishonouring God, and am wretched
in myself by living as I do, and that I *must* either go backwards
or forwards, reaching out towards the light and the glory which
my blessed Saviour holds out to me, or falling back more and
more into worldliness and sin." Accordingly he came to the
Oxford Convention, and we shall never forget the tremulous
tone in which he spoke to us there. His words, as recorded in
his life, and as given with some abridgment in our account of
the wonderful Oxford gatherings, made an impression both deep
and lasting. Still more lasting was the impression made by
the saintly life that followed. It seemed to be an echo
of his farewell words there,—" Sing unto the Lord a new
song every day ; an old one will not do, for His mercies are new
every morning." At the Friday night prayer meeting, he
spoke of the Conference, and of the happy results in his own
experience. Some remember the glow which overspread his
face, telling, apart from his words, of some new secret that
had " illuminated his life." In this spirit he sent an address
to the Annual Conference of the Evangelical Union for the
Diocese. In this spirit he testified again at Brighton.

This was the man, marked out by God to gather an ever-
widening circle of people " convicted for holiness," and of
others who, hardly sharing that conviction, came under the
spell and then sought and found the secret of sanctification.
This was the man spiritually, morally, mentally, socially, physically fitted by God to be the Moses to lead His people out of
Egypt. The more those who gather at Keswick are " baptized with the same Spirit," the more will it be what its founders
projected—see their invitation—" a meeting for the promotion of practical holiness."

Side by side with Canon Battersby there always stands in
memory the massive figure of Mr. Robert Wilson, a member of
the Society of Friends. His nonconformity was not only no
barrier, but supplied the one element else awanting in the
foundation of a united and uniting effort for Christians of all
Churches. " He was the selecter," says Dr. Elder Cumming,

" of the Keswick Motto ' All one in Christ Jesus,' and was responsible, for the three flags, ' Love—Joy—Peace,' which fly over the Tent. His love for prayer (and *habits* of prayer) was great, he was always finding or making excuses for special prayer, and it was very striking to mark his words when we prayed together alone. He was a great strength to Canon Battersby at the beginning of the Keswick story. It is hardly too much to say that without Mr. Wilson's support and backing, there would have been no Keswick story at all."

It ought also to be noticed that while the Canon was a Cumbrian only by adoption, his colleague was one by birth. The hamlet of Broughton Grange, not far from Cockermouth, was a settlement of early Baptists and early Friends—Mr. Wilson being one of the latter. There was no Parish Church until about a century ago. Mr. Wilson did everything to promote harmony amongst all. A visitor asked to what church he belonged ; and a resident replied,—" he goes to the Friends' Meeting in the morning, to the Baptist Chapel in the afternoon, and to the Parish Church in the evening."

So that when Canon Battersby suggested a Convention of Christians of every name, our friend was quite in his element. He could be firm, but he could not be unkind, and his uniting spirit showed a wonderful power for the cohesion of " a fortuitous concourse of atoms." Genial as he was good, " he exercised a large and liberal hospitality, by which the public work of the Convention was furthered not a little."

Such were the scenes and such were the men wherein and whereby God planted a sapling which has grown into a spreading tree, under whose shadow thousands have sat with great delight and found its fruit sweet unto their taste.

The sapling was small enough at first, so small that the editors of papers took very little notice of it. Why should they ? Keswick was a quieter spot than Cambridge, or Nottingham, or Hull, or a score of other places, where Conventions were held that year. Editors are not prophets, and could not foresee " unto what this would grow." Hence the accounts of this epoch-making gathering are meagre in the extreme. *The Pathway of Power*, now known as *The Life of Faith*,—gives but a couple of columns in all,—they are from the pen of Canon Battersby,—descriptive of this historic meeting.

The Christian of that date gives one column consisting of a letter of Canon Battersby's, similar to that in *The Pathway*,[1] and another by H. F. B. Next year, 1876, I can find no notice in *The Christian*. In 1877, there is one column, in which the united character of the gathering is brought out by reference to the presence of the Bishop of Sydney amongst ministers of various denominations. Some months after the first Convention, one and another of those who attended seem to have recalled the fact that they had notebooks, and to have sent extracts therefrom to the Editor of *The Pathway of Power*.

Taking part in the Convention from the first, and but for two occasions of illness personal or relative, always there to the present time was the Rev. (now Preb.) W. H. Webb-Peploe. It is deeply interesting to have from him an account of this first Convention.[2] " On arriving in Keswick, we went straight to the Tent, which had in it a gathering of three or four hundred people. Canon Battersby was, of course, the leader, while Mr. Robert Wilson, with wonderful self-denial, undertook all the arrangements. During the days of Convention our numbers may have reached, at some meetings, 600 ; but of the great gatherings now expected we knew nothing then. I had only gone as a listener, but like others found myself called to speak almost all day long, owing to the absence of those who had been expected as leaders." All that the speakers knew of " preparation times " was that after long and earnest prayer, in Canon Battersby's house at night, he would apportion next day's work, and say to each one, ' Will you take this ? ' and ' Will you take that ? ' No one thought of questioning his appointment, but took it as being directly ' of the Lord.' "

How good it is to reflect that this brave servant of Christ, who has stood for a generation and more as one of the polished corners of the Temple in the great metropolis, has been for a similar period one of the props of the Tent at Keswick. His fearlessness, his unrivalled knowledge of the Word of God, his wonderful memory of its inmost treasures, his mellifluous voice, and a certain atmosphere of *distinction* about his presence combine to give him a unique place in the work of the sanctuary. Of course we all feel that he ought to have been made a Bishop. As a clergyman once said to the present writer,

---

[1] Given on a later page. [2] See Dr. Harford's book.

" It will be an eternal disgrace to the Church of England if
Canon Hoare and the Rev. James Vaughan are not advanced
to the Bench," so he might have said of the Prebendary. But
when one thinks of what London is to England, and the West
End to London, one is more than doubtful whether any office
or any honour could have been greater than to have stood for
all these years in Belgravia, and there still " to flourish like the
palm tree and grow as a cedar of Lebanon."

In *The Pathway* of January, 1876, the notes are given of one
of this great teacher's addresses delivered at Keswick six
months before. " It is the question of the Christian's Walk
which we meet to discuss, not any new doctrine or phase of
religion. In 1 Thessalonians ii. 11–13 St. Paul shows us
the object, the measure, and the ground of the Christian's walk.
' Walk worthy of God.' This is the whole object of our
teaching in these solemn gatherings, because we believe that
God has called us to be conformed to the image of His Son.
Perfectly it cannot be until we stand before Him in glory,
but we have yet to learn how far it may be attained in this
life. He hath called us unto fellowship with His Son. There
is something wrong with us if it is not so. In Ephesians i. 4,
we are told that God hath called us to be holy *now*." Many
texts were quoted and elucidated by the speaker in his well-
known manner. " So far, the purpose of God the Father in
calling us. Note, now the purpose of the Son in dying to
redeem us ; was it simply to take away our guilt, and leave
us to walk with shuffling gait, which might make Godless ones
mock at our claim to salvation ? No, He died that they
which live, should not henceforth live unto themselves, but
unto Him who died for them." Here another pile of texts was
reared up. Again, what was the purpose of God the Spirit
in descending to earth to take possession of our souls ? That
we might be " changed into the same image, the image of
Christ." Another series of texts followed this. " You and I
have slandered the blessed Word of God, by doubting whether
such things were possible." But as St. Paul says of the Thessalonians so may it be said of all now present : " When ye received
the Word of God, ye received it not as the word of man, but as
it is in truth, the word of God, which effectually worketh also in
you that believe."

Other speakers at the first Convention were the Revs. G. R.
Thornton, and Thomas Phillips, three very able laymen, Mr.
Bowker, Mr. Croome and Mr. Murray Shipley, and at the ladies'
meetings Mrs. Compton. This dear sister in Christ still
lives and still delights in " whatsoever things are pure, lovely,
and of good report."

The others have all passed away. The Rev. G. R. Thornton
came of a notable family whose pious father was called home
early, but who had been trained with unusual care by a mother
as able as she was consecrated. Two or three of the sons went
into the ministry, and one, a layman, is foremost in every good
work in and about Nottingham. The daughters had their
Mission Hall, and the influence of such a family and its many
branches is wide-spread and beautiful. The Rev. George
Thornton, the essence of kindliness and geniality, did a
good work at Bengeo, and then for years at his beautiful Church
in Kensington. As one of those whose words at Oxford
brought Canon Battersby into liberty it is natural to hear of
his being asked to Keswick. Mr. Croome, brother-in-law of
Mr. Webb-Peploe, deeply taught in the truth of sanctification,
brought all the resources of an acute legal mind to deal with
the questions. And Mr. Bowker, an Evangelical of the Evangelicals, was the very man to answer questions, solve difficulties, and remove prejudices.

The notes of addresses of Mr. Murray Shipley's are striking,—
" The Holy Spirit dwells in every one of God's children, and
the promise is ' Ye shall have power.' If then we have the
Holy Ghost, what hinders the power ? Look at that locomotive
all ready to start, and yet it stands still. Some little wedge in
front needs to be removed ; so something hinders God's
operations in my heart. What is it ? Lord search me ! Little
sins are little foxes that spoil the vines. Great sins we *do* put
away, but the voluntary surrender of little sins, those which
even the *Christian* world does not condemn, and with it
whole-hearted consecration to God are the things needed that
we may realise God's power in our souls. Depend not on
the act of surrender or consecration but on Christ Himself for
supplies of grace every moment. If you want to teach a little
child to write, you hold his hand and tell him to yield it to
yours. If he obeys then every one will recognise the hand-

writing as yours. So ' Yield yourselves to God ; ' let Christ in you do His own work and people will see that God is writing His will in your actions."

The next day there came striking illustrations from Joshua ; showing how the Lord took—gave—sent—brought—destroyed —delivered. Lingering over the last thought, Mr. Shipley said, " I must ever look to the smitten Rock for power, and trace up all deliverance to the death and resurrection of the Lord Jesus Christ. We may have wanted a clearer mental conception of how we are delivered, but I have learned that I have greater strength and victory by realizing Christ as my present Saviour *this* moment, and then the *next* moment, without thinking how it is so—not relying on *thought*, but on *Him*. It is not by taking up, as it were, a sponge full of water in the morning, to last through the day, but realizing Him as the living spring in my heart, moment by moment, delivering me from this little temper or that great temptation." From one of the headlands of our American coast, during a great tempest, I saw the wrecks of ten vessels, while not one ship in the harbour was damaged. If our whole being, spirit, soul, and body, is anchored on Jesus, then self will abdicate the throne and give place to Jesus, that He may reign in and over us as a present Saviour from sin.

Canon Battersby in *The Pathway of Power*, August, 1875, writes : " The Lord has answered us according to our faith, even beyond our faith. A wonderful blessing has attended our meetings, and hundreds have gone away rejoicing in Christ, as the Healer and Restorer of their souls. The announcement, at the last moment almost, that those to whom we had looked for the chief guidance of the meetings could not attend, sent us, in a very urgent and expectant mood, to the throne of Grace, and we pleaded there, as the man in the parable (Luke xii. 5–8) did, with our Divine ' Friend ' for the help we so much needed. And He gave it. Other helpers came in answer to our telegrams and their presence in the power of the Holy Ghost, Who most manifestly spoke by their lips, fully supplied our need.

At the first meeting in the tent, Monday evening, June 28, the key-note was struck, which vibrated through all the later meetings, from Psalm lxii., ' My soul, wait thou only upon God, for my expectation is from Him.' In this holy expecta- tion we were kept from day to day, from hour to hour ; and the

Divine Presence was as surely in our tent as in the tabernacle of old when He dwelt behind the veil, only that for us the veil was withdrawn. On Tuesday, Wednesday, Thursday, and Friday, we met at 7 a.m. for prayer and praise, and truly refreshing were those morning hours, when the dew of heaven fell so abundantly on the spirits of some three or four hundred worshippers who gathered at those times to wait upon God.

The culminating point was reached, it may be said, in the noon meeting on Thursday, July 1, when the subject of the Holy Ghost, as ' the promise of the Father ' to the Church, was brought forward. Some who before had ' doubted whereunto this would grow,' were unable any longer to withstand the power of the truth which was then pressed upon them, and a holy awe seemed to rest on all."

Another writer on the same page adds—" It is impossible to describe the holy awe which pervaded the large assembly on that Thursday morning, as the work of the Holy Spirit was presented together with the command, ' BE FILLED WITH THE SPIRIT ! ' and especially, perhaps, during those minutes when, in solemn stillness, we asked the Lord that henceforth we might neither be *barren nor unfruitful* in the knowledge of our Lord Jesus Christ ! "

Besides testimonies given at the time others were received afterwards indicating " the ability to make a full surrender to the Lord, and the consequent experience of an abiding peace, exceeding far anything previously experienced." " Such results, attained under circumstances which might have been expected to throw a considerable amount of discouragement over the meetings, may," says Canon Battersby, " serve to encourage us, and others too, with more and more boldness, to press upon all who name the name of Christ, the full privilege to which they are called."

As we have heard people, who had the privilege of gathering round the saintly William Pennefather in his suburban parish, speak of the Barnet Conferences as having a freshness and sweetness which the far larger gatherings at Mildmay, to their apprehension, seemed to lack ; so, we can imagine, that the privileged few who attended the first Keswick Convention would feel that no later Convention, however large, quite came up to it. Those who had gathered had come very specially for blessing, some of them indeed, had already found it, and the rest we fancy, almost to a man, had come resolved not to go away without it. " The Lord God was with them ; and the shout of a King was amongst them." If we are right in considering that such was the temper of those who thus solemnly assembled themselves together, we need not wonder that they went away blessed and to be a blessing.

Some had come from distant parts of England, Scotland, and Ireland, if not farther still, and all, we are sure, went home as with winged feet the bearers of glad tidings to multitudes all around. Their testimony of what they had heard and seen and felt was calculated to produce, and, as we know, did produce, a great and widespread expectation.

The " circumstances of discouragement " to which Canon Battersby refers were doubtless the absence of the leader of former gatherings of the kind, but the former gatherings were not convened by local invitation. That at Keswick was ; and it was as natural that the Vicar of the Parish, on whose grounds moreover the " Tent of Meeting " was pitched, should be Chairman at Keswick, as that Mr. Pearsall Smith should act in that capacity at Oxford and Brighton. He had retired to his home in Philadelphia in grievously shattered health. Such serious illness, to use the words of one [1] who knew Mr. Smith intimately, overtook him, and from that period he was practically withdrawn from public life, and the leadership of the Movement naturally fell into the hands of the Vicar of St. John's, Keswick, and his friend—and everybody's friend—Mr. Robert Wilson. That was as far as Meetings in Cumberland were concerned. Elsewhere the forces for " the deepening of the spiritual life " rallied round Mr. Bowker—that phrase was his discovery. He gathered meetings in the West End of London, and later in Brighton, in Dublin, and in Edinburgh. He was asked also to preside at many of the Conventions organized by others, as in Cheltenham and York. He had much to do with the direction, while the Reverend Evan Hopkins was Editor, of *The Life of Faith* and other publications to spread the light ; and to Mr. Bowker's wise steering the good ship owed, under God, much of its prosperous voyage.

Ah, they were good old times, the days of those early Con-

[1] A much-esteemed clergyman in the Metropolis.

ventions ! Never shall we forget the seven o'clock prayer
meetings in the dark winter mornings at Hull, and the last
evening meeting there with Dr. Matthew Robertson's ringing
words " Let us part cheerfully." Cheerfully indeed we did
part next morning, when the Rev. John Deck, and quite a
little crowd, saw us off by the early train.

So there were men whose faith failed not, and whose courage
never faltered. Little do we know, now that the Movement
has its settled basis and wide ramifications, how much we owe
to these brave and believing men.

To revert to the absence of the Chairman of the Oxford and
Brighton meetings. In a letter to the author on a spiritual
subject, Mrs. Pearsall Smith makes the following touching
allusion :—

> " Mr. Smith's health is very poor, and he is obliged to live a very
> quiet and domestic life. He thinks he cannot live long, but, of course,
> this is something we know nothing about. Some physicians say that
> he has a very serious heart trouble. I believe myself that the springs
> of his life were sapped in 1874, and that existence can never be any-
> thing but weariness and suffering to him again in this world. In the
> next, he will renew his youth, I am sure, and be happy once more. For
> myself, *I am at rest in God.* I say this in its profoundest meaning.
> My soul is *satisfied* in Him."
>
> " Yours warmly,
" H. W. SMITH.
>
> "PHILADELPHIA, PA.,
> *March* 29, 1883."

One cannot make what may be a last allusion to this gracious
and gifted woman, without adding that her usefulness by no
means ended when her appearance on Convention platforms
ceased. Papers from her pen appeared almost every month
in *The Pathway of Power*, while her *Christian's Secret of a Happy
Life*, *Everyday Religion*, and other books did more than any
publications ever written to extend the knowledge of the truth
of sanctification. She did also occasionally advocate this
subject in public,—though her more frequent appearances were
in the cause of temperance.

At a Convention at Broadlands years after, at which it was
the author's privilege to be present, her words had the old
inspiring ring ; and so the last time we heard her in public, in a

spiritual address she gave at the Friends' Meeting House, in Brighton.   The glow of joy and peace was no less manifest in private, when during her widowhood we used to visit her in London.

After she left Town for Oxford, we heard equally cheering expressions from attached friends, and a printed letter of her own, sent round privately about a month before she went home to God, tells the same tale. " Some of you may want to know," she writes, " just how I am, and what are my surroundings.   I am living with my son and my two granddaughters in a beautiful house on the banks of the Thames, not far from Oxford, with frequent visits from my daughter Mary from Italy, and at least a weekly visit from my daughter Alys, now living in Cambridge.   I could not ask for a lovelier refuge in which to pass the last years of my life, nor for better company. I am, as no doubt you all know, very much of an invalid, and am obliged to sit in a wheeled chair both day and night, as my many infirmities prevent me from much lying in bed, but I am very comfortable in my chair and get plenty of sleep.   I cannot either read or write much, and often am not well enough to see my friends.   In fact, I have very little energy for anything, and am not even able to go on with a half-finished book that I was in the midst of writing when I was taken ill.   My old activities have all had to be laid aside, and I am only waiting and longing for the blessed call to my heavenly home, but I am glad to tell you that I am very happy and contented in my narrowed life, and with my lessening capabilities, and can say ' Thy will be done ' to my divine Master from the very bottom of my heart."

After an incident of an old negress, Nancy, Mrs. Smith continues,—

" Do not think for a moment that this is because Nancy and I are extra good and pious people, for we are not at all, but just like most of the Christians around us, and probably not half so good and pious as many, but we have found from the Lord Jesus three things about God which have convinced us that it is to our best interest to trust and obey Him :—God is wise : God is good : God is love.   And what more could we ask of the God whom we are commanded to worship and trust and obey than that he should be just this ; wise and good and loving ? Dear Friends, is this the character we attribute to our God ? This splendid, magnificent character that once to know must enchain our hearts for ever. Why, dear friends, if we did really believe that our God was this sort of God we should all be millionaires of grace ; nay, multi-millionaires. Nancy and I do believe it, and we *are* multi-millionaires ; rich in nothing of our own, but rich beyond words in the wisdom and goodness and love of our God. ' Thou, O God, art all we want ; more than all in Thee we find.' This God is our God, and He is enough. This is my greeting for 1911, and since it is so late, a birthday greeting as well, as I was 79 a few days ago. May all to whom I send this message say—Amen and Amen.

" Yours in Christ,
" H. W. PEARSALL SMITH."

A little later this happy spirit took its flight. The daughter, spoken of above, had left the room with the doctor, and on her return the patient asked, " What news ? " When she learned that the end was coming, she replied with a smile, " Good ! " And so—

" On God's own will she laid her down
As child upon a mother's breast,"

and now a small urn contains all of her that is left to earth ; she herself is " numbered with " God's " saints in glory everlasting."

Through the kindness of her daughter, the Hon. Mrs. Russell, we have been favoured with the perusal of a book, not yet on English shelves—*A Quaker Grandmother*, by Ray Strachey. Fleming Revell Co. A first glance showed only the happy portrait of one growing young again in the youth around her. But reading the book through we often found deeper notes—grief for the gulf between her and those brought up in their father's Church (the Roman Catholic), but above all her intense realization and joy in God.

Delighting in the presence of her grandchildren—and in their pranks—nevertheless, when circumstances took them far away, she could write thus :—

" No matter what loved ones may come or go, I feel always that the home of my soul is never for one instant disturbed. God is always the one supreme passion of my heart and possessing Him I can do without all besides." And the granddaughter adds, " This was not merely the ideal she strove for. It was the literal fact." "*O si sic omnes !* "

CHAPTER VI

"WHAT TIME THE STORM FELL UPON THEE"

" Oh, what a God is He
On whom our faith relies !
So full of power, so full of love,
So tender and so wise.

" His one divine command
The stormy wind can raise ;
Held in the hollow of His hand,
He speaks and it obeys.

" So calm or storm are sent
As tokens of His love,
To draw us closer yet to Him,
To raise our hearts above."

ANNIE W. MARSTON.

IN July, 1876, we paid a first visit to Lakeland. A break
in the clouds after a day of rain led Mr. Sampson, of
Hull, with whom I shared rooms, to hurry me away, after
some refreshment, to have a look at Derwentwater under a
wild sky, in which bars of crimson foretold coming storm.
So we wended our way to Friars Crag, the spot visited by so
many thousands since.

The portended storm fell during the time of the Convention,
giving us, in Canon Battersby's words, " weather the most
adverse—excessive rain with thunder and lightning, and
violent gusts of wind resulting on the third day in the over-
throw of our beautiful tent." But the promise " Thou wilt
keep him in perfect peace, whose mind is stayed on Thee,"
was abundantly realized in the experience of all concerned.

The hurricane of that night was such that it was with
extreme thankfulness one found himself outside the frail tent,
a very different one from the stouter fabrics now erected there.
After the last meeting that evening, both cords and canvas had

been strained to the utmost, and it seemed as though the tent might at any moment collapse, leaving the great congregation buried under its folds. Mercifully, it was not till about midnight that the tempest snapped the ropes and levelled the tent to the ground. Was the Convention suspended ? Not for an hour. When—all unconscious of what had happened—we issued forth for the seven o'clock morning meeting, we saw large posters, telling us where that meeting, and all the meetings, would be held ; schoolrooms, lecture rooms, and every place then available (it was long before " the Pavilion," and other " Halls " were built) being placed at our service. We were given to understand that Mr. Wilson, called from his bed, had aroused the printers to get out posters ; and so by morning everything was in order.

The principal speakers included those of the previous year with the addition of Mrs. Johnson, Mrs. Wightman, the Revs. J. E. Sampson, R. B. Girdlestone, and Evan H. Hopkins. This last speaker has been called "the theologian of the Convention," and most certainly his insight into divine truth, his careful scrutiny of the Scriptures bearing upon sanctification, his lucid definitions and distinctions, his equally lucid illustrations of the great truths he seeks to enforce, have made him an invaluable teacher. More than any man he has kept the Movement from being drawn into extravagance or excitement. How often and how greatly his skilful steering amid shoals and quicksands has been needed that the vessel might hold on steadfastly its straight and scriptural course ! Never getting very far away from the groundwork, he has more than once referred to what came to him " at a small meeting in London in May, 1873." He has retained that experience with remarkable . tenacity, and has patiently sought to lead others to the enjoyment of similar blessing. Those who have been privileged to know him in his own home, or to hear him in private gatherings, will also be aware of what the outer public know nothing—an intensity even unto tears with which this "ambassador for Christ " is sometimes charged in delivering his message.

Canon Battersby speaks of the intense blessedness of the early morning prayer meetings, and adds that " the conversational side-meetings, in which opportunity was given for the free discussion of all questions connected with the subjects handled by the speakers, were invariably crowded with hearers, eager to have their difficulties solved." He adds that " the beautiful hymns in Mr. Mountain's collection contributed not a little to the devotional part of the services and seemed to lift us sensibly heavenwards."

A much fuller account appears in *The Pathway of Power* concerning the Convention of 1877. It is evidently a record by a very skilful hand. The date was, as in all subsequent years, the last complete week of July. " Only those who have seen mountain rain falling for hours, as it rarely pours for minutes elsewhere, will understand how earnest was the desire for fine weather. Gratefully, therefore, under gleams of sunshine," the large congregation gathered at Monday evening's meeting. Praise opened the Convention, as it closed with praise. The first words of prayer were those which the Lord taught us to pray, solemnly breathed from the lips of all. Canon Battersby expressed in David's words (Psalm lxii.) the attitude of the assembly : " Truly my soul waiteth upon God ; from Him cometh my Salvation." The Rev. E. H. Hopkins, through Ephesians i., pressed upon us a definite and individual seeking of blessing.

Mr. Bowker, after a time of prayer, rose as one who could attest the truth " He is able." " We come," he said, " with testimonies of victories, but as Abraham would receive no gifts from the king of Sodom, because he had been blessed by Melchizedek, so we would disclaim everything ourselves, as we owe everything to Christ."

Thus at the opening meeting, in the words of one [1] who by name and birth is closely linked to Keswick—

Christ is the end, for Christ was the beginning ;
Christ the beginning, for the end is Christ.

The first prayer meeting was opened by prayer by Messrs. M. Wallis and H. Bowker. In other meetings an interesting feature was the reading of a chapter by the President, without comment. The addresses were many of them simple expositions of the Word, and everything showed that the Bible held its true place amongst us as the interpreter of God to man.

[1] Frederic Myers.

Conversational meetings were exceedingly interesting and animated times. Messrs. Charles Braithwaite and Thomas Fisher assisted the ordinary leaders in these meetings, of which the writer, whose record we are rigorously condensing, adds ; " We might fill pages with jottings here, but can only give one or two examples. ' Does the Spirit's presence uniformly inspire the soul with very warm feeling ? ' ' I cannot tell how the Spirit enters. As the fire gets into a cold bar of iron, and makes it glow until we can hardly tell which is iron and which is fire, so the Holy Spirit flows into the heart, and makes a burning and a shining light of some rough-hewn man ; but it is impossible to say anything about the " how " in either case.' ' Is conflict incongruous with perfect peace and joy ? ' ' There is no disagreement between the two. We have rest *in* troubles here ; we shall have rest *from* trouble by and by. God can say *to* the waves, ' Peace, be still ; ' or He can say *in* the waves, ' It is I, be not afraid.' "

The Ladies' Meetings were conducted by Mrs. Michael Baxter. " Though," says one, " she made me thoroughly ashamed of my slovenly Christianity, I felt at the same time how noble my little life could be ; yes, I may say humbly, *shall* be, in the strength of Jesus. Few who were present will forget the impressive and heart-searching words which were given her to speak, or the expression of her happy heaven-lighted face as she dwelt on what manner of persons we ought to be."

Referring to guidance, she said : " We know the Shepherd speaks, but sometimes we do not get into the direct line of His voice—the line of *sacrifice* and of *trust*. We too often say, ' Lord, teach us to do Thy will, but I do want to do my own.' "

Mr. Marriage Wallis, well-known in Brighton especially, and honoured wherever known, speaking in the general meeting, dealt with the defeat at Ai, illustrating it by reference to Psalm xxxii., and also the words of the beloved disciple, " If we confess our sins, He is faithful and just to forgive us our sins." " Those who, like myself," he said, " are continually mingling with the world, know how hard it is to keep their garments pure. I feel great sympathy with such ; and I can tell you from my own experience that God does keep His children, even in the midst of business cares and perplexities. May I give you a word of hearty encouragement to trust to God to keep you, moment by moment ! " A season of earnest prayer followed, led by Mr. Wilson, and then the humble confession broke forth, " There is sin in the camp . . . is it, O Lord, in me ? " We trace the ordered progress, guided by the Holy Spirit, when next morning the Rev. E. H. Hopkins expanded the same theme more fully from words in 1st John, and later from 1 Corinthians i. 30, the Bishop of Sydney previously leading in prayer.

Again the hallowed spirit of prayer fell over the meeting as Mr. Thomas Whitwell knelt to present our petition, to be immediately afterwards exchanged for united praise—

"On Thee my heart is resting."

The subject of the indwelling home of the Spirit was introduced by Dr. Hodgson, of Liverpool. " Stephen, a man filled with the Holy Ghost, shot far ahead of his companions. His dream of quiet usefulness in the service of Christ is soon dissipated. Dragged before the Sanhedrin, the living God was within him, beaming forth in the radiancy of his face. The very character of his Lord is in his prayer for his murderers. Would we be successful in works of usefulness, would we have our faces shine with sublime faith, and die full of joy and triumph, we must be filled with the Spirit."

Mr. Isaac Brown, of Kendal, dealing with the terms often used amongst us said : " The principle meaning of righteousness is being right, or rather, being *righted*. As we have to turn to the Latin and say ' justify ' for ' counting right,' so we have, to say ' sanctify ' for ' making holy.' ' Sanctify Christ in your hearts as Lord ' (1 Peter iii. 15). Holiness, therefore, consists in putting ourselves into Christ's hands, and truly owning Him supreme."

At the closing meeting " came one of those sweet seasons of communion when, at the President's invitation, some ten minutes were spent in giving the present experience of God's goodness in a verse of Scripture. Rapidly from side to side arose the tide of thanksgiving—' Henceforth let no man trouble me, for I bear in my body the marks of the Lord Jesus.' ' Thou hast loosed my bonds.' ' Bless me, even me also, O my Father.'

" The following Sunday many echoed the text of the beloved President—' This is the Lord's doing, and it is marvellous in our eyes.' Having learnt our way into the sanctuary, let us be increasingly taught the other side of the priest's office ; when he came forth thence to give hope to the leper, to release the bondsman, and to teach redemption through death and sacrifice."

The hurricane which blew down the Tent this year was perhaps symbolic of the tornado of opinion which blew around the Movement for a lengthened period. But he knows not the value of an oak who knows nothing of the storms it has weathered. It is not the cursory passer-by who admires its foliage, or the tired traveller who rests under its shadow, but the herdsman out in all seasons, out in the tranquil hour, and out also when the hurricane plays havoc in the forest, who appreciates the tree sprung from the acorn. The oak's tenacity of life it is that proves its Creator's power, and shows that the tree is the possessor of a " life which is life indeed."

That text is the title of a volume as we saw, on one of the earliest gatherings of the Movement we are tracing—the Conference at Broadlands.

How sweet and calm were its hours ! How gracious too the outburst of glory and beauty at Oxford ! We in Brighton also had another memorable Convention ; but, hardly had its meetings ended, when the storm broke.

The wind blew from many quarters. There are those who dislike every departure from ordinary routine. There are others who, to speak frankly, give occasion for this dislike by extreme sentiments, and by language which has more of hyperbole than truth. The former might be disregarded, the latter were " thorns in " our " sides " ; very sharp they were, and very painful the wounds they gave. They were in many a case " the wounds of a friend," but none the less painful on that account.

But it was from the opposite quarter that at that time the tempest had to be encountered. The organs of orthodoxy sent forth utterances of alarm. If but a new phrase were introduced the stalwarts trembled as though the earth reeled under their feet. No word in the theological dictionary was too bad for the Movement. It was " Perfectionism," it was " sinlessness " it was " rank heresy." And after all it was introduced by one man—call it after him, call it " Pearsall Smithism," and " down with it, down with it, even to the ground." All this was hard to bear. It seems easy now, now that the organs of opinion have changed their tunes,[1] much as the nation has done about the Salvation Army, since King Edward and Queen Alexandra showed their generous interest in it. But it was a different matter in those days ; a different and a difficult matter for Evangelical Churchmen, and for Nonconformists too, to bear being battered with the brickbats of heresy-hunters ; and not by such only, by any means, but by dear godly men, jealous for what seemed to them the very truth of Heaven.

Yet those who were assailed stood firm ; they "knew Whom " they "had believed, and were persuaded that " the core of this matter was a rod out of the stem of Holy Scripture, watered by the very Spirit of God. So they stood at the parting of the ways, neither carried off by the fanaticism of the extremists, nor cooled in their ardour by the chilling reception their testimony met from the pillars of orthodoxy.

Yes, the oak bore test after test, and flourished and bore fruit, even "such time as when the storm fell upon " it.

Those who crowd the tents of happy Keswick to-day, can hardly tell how much it cost their fathers to gather there at all, and should honour those fathers (and above all revere the truth round which they rallied) all the more for the brave stand they made. Thinking over their steadfastness and faith, and dwelling upon the truth of God and "the immutability of His counsel," we might almost use the words Byron wrote about his daughter, and call the Keswick Convention—

> " The Child of love, though born in bitterness,
> And nurtured in convulsion."

---

[1] The Press—and the religious Press is no exception—must needs be in the van of opinion, and express it in the strongest terms. This implies no real bitterness, and there are instances—and here is a notable one—when the Press comes round nobly, and gives unstinted praise to that for which it once had nothing but blame.

CHAPTER VII

NEW VOICES FROM FAR AND NEAR

"I am with you alway."

"Thou great ' I Am ' still with me ! O what strength,
What fellowship in that o'ershadowing fame !
Angels that wait on Thee will ask my name,
And wonder Thou dost commune at such length
With creature so unworthy. Tell them, Lord,
I was a poor dependant once of Thine,
With name so tarnished that Thou said'st, ' Take mine,'
And bid me to Thy house, and heart, and board !
' I Am ' of human story ! Thou'rt the same
That walked with prophet and with patriarch
In the world's twilight, while it yet was dark ;
Creation's dawn fresh echoing back ' I Am ' !
Twilight and dark still linger here—O call,
Call home my proud will, life's last prodigal ! "

CHARLES A. FOX.

NOTHING is more characteristic of Keswick than the wide circle from which it draws its teachers. They come not only from different churches, but from different countries. Many a time an Irish or Scotch voice has followed the English note, yet not so often but that " the predominant partner " holds its own. And gallant little Wales would not be left out, since .Dr. Griffith Thomas and Mrs. Penn Lewis came to speak to many hearts and minds, and when the wave of blessing broke over the Principality some of its refreshing spray reached our tents.

There has been a beautiful interchange between England and America here. Africa has served us well ; while bishops and missionaries by the score have come from India, China, Persia and elsewhere. Nor must we forget our brethren of other nationalties. In the earliest days many felt as though no convention were complete without the presence of Pastors Monod and

Stockmeyer. Distinguished visitors, if not teachers, have often come from Holland. Russia has sent us some of her notables. The late Queen of Sweden and Prince Oscar have graced our assemblies : in the more private meetings, it was an inspiration to hear the earnest humility of the Prince's prayers.

In 1878 there appeared on the scene for the first time one who used to be a welcome visitor for a score of years or more. He came from the ends of the earth, for he was then a vicar in Melbourne and son of its Dean. But the present writer cannot but claim him as representing Ireland as well as Australia ; not only his surname, Macartney, but his christian names, Hussey Burgh, recalled men well-known in Irish story. Sent home to study at Trinity College, Dublin, he returned to Australia half a century ago. Voyages were long in those days, and two manuscript newspapers were published on that ship. They were afterwards printed, and copies are in the possession of a Brighton doctor ! It is delightful to find that our friend, while entering into all the innocent life of the ship, was, though as yet unordained, voted to the place of chaplain, and took services and Bible classes.

So soon as the Movement began, Australia " caught on." Cauldfield, of which Mr. Macartney had become Vicar, distinguished itself in two ways—by the generosity of its gifts to Foreign Missions, and by holding a Convention for the promotion of holiness.

It is not very surprising after this to learn that its vicar longed to visit England and Ireland, and especially to attend meetings in different centres in which the fire that had fallen from heaven was kindled and cherished. On our friend's visiting England, it was felt at once that he had perhaps more to teach than to learn. It was our hap first to meet him at a Cheltenham Convention ; there he made deep impression. Addresses of his at Mildmay left the same mark. Deep Celtic fervour, profound knowledge of the Word of God, intense devotion to the Person of the Lord Jesus, and the practise of private prayer to an unwonted extent, accounted for the influence he wielded.

Mr. Macartney's impressions of the religious life of these countries, on that and a subsequent visit, were given in letters to a Melbourne paper, afterwards published under the strange title of *England, Home and Beauty*. Dr. Eugene Stock has

characterized these volumes as containing most valuable
sketches of the religious history of the last quarter of the
nineteenth century. The two persons that stand out most
vividly on these pages are Father Ignatius and Mr. Robert
Chapman, of Barnstaple. What a contrast! But the spirit
that wrote—

"Let me come closer to Thee, Jesus."

was akin to Macartney's, and with all his "faults he loved him
still." But his love was not blind, and he felt impelled to go
and see Ignatius and remonstrate with him about many things.
There was no similar exception to be taken to the teaching of
the author of *Choice Sayings*; while the life of Mr. Chapman,
more beautiful even than his words, grappled Mr. Macartney
to his heart as with hooks of steel. It will be easily understood that the appearing at Keswick of this noteworthy
Australian clergyman made a deep impression. Accordingly
we are not surprised to read in *The Pathway of Power*,
"Morning after morning the people assembled early and
gathered the manna which truly the Lord gave them.
The words then were chiefly from the Rev. H. B. Macartney,
which for their freshness, simplicity and unction seemed to
have come straight from the One Shepherd." And notes of
those words are appended, the only notes in *The Pathway* of
the addresses of that year.

The first morning the address was from Canticles v. 2–8,
"Christ will come—not to be a stranger, just looking in and
hurrying away. But oh, is it not wonderful that Christ, who
has all the business of the universe in His hands, has leisure for
you!" "I have put off my coat, how shall I put it on; I
have washed my feet, how shall I defile them? There are
times when we *don't want* the Lord Jesus—we don't want HIM,
but *He wants us*—yes, and He wants *you*, not the myrrh. . .
There must be 'nothing between.' If you sin, go back to the
Lord Jesus *like lightning*; go to Him, sin and all; go to Him
without your graces, because He alone can give the graces
that please His Heavenly Father."

The second address was from Romans vii. 4, "Married to
Another." "The law was always saying 'Thou shalt,' and
'we could not'—it was not in us. But Christ does not say

' Thou shalt,' but ' I will.' . . . I believe the blessing of to-day
will be putting aside all other things, and going *into God* to see
what God is. God cannot be known by those who are always
ill at ease or in a hurry. . . . I don't know a more blessed
position than just to wait outside our Bridegroom's chamber,
and through the open door to hear Him making mention of us.
. . . It is better to overhear the Lord Jesus telling God about
you, or, to let Him tell you yourself. If we do not listen to the
voice of Jesus, some one else less friendly will tell us." Speaking on Philippians iii. 3, he began in . this striking way :
" Do you know that the Tempter has been up early this morning, and that he is now abroad saying that this is the last day
of the Convention—therefore take your pleasure and let go
prayer ? . . . What is the Father's joy ? Just one word—
Jesus. You look at your own heart, and perhaps you find
no love there. What are you to do ? Ask God to give you
some of His own love for His Son. The highest Christian life
is to get our souls flooded with love for Jesus from the Father's
heart. We forget the Spirit so much, and yet we owe Him
everything. Think of ' the love of the Spirit ' ; think lovingly
of the gentle absent One, sent by the Father, and sent by the
Son, to win and to adorn the Bride. . . . Nothing gives so much
gladness in Hell as the believer's sin. Put away everything of
the nature of sin. Our sins wound the Lord Jesus ; they
wounded Him long ago in the body, and now they wound Him
in the soul."

From 2 Kings iv. 4, with Canticles i. 9, he said : " I have
compared thee, O my love, to a company of horses in Pharaoh's
chariots." " Look at those dark black arabs, a man at the
head of each to hold them back ! Are you like that company
of steeds in Pharaoh's chariot ? Are you ready to do—ready
to die ? And these horses are war horses—they go, not where
they like, but where they are driven ; and we go, not where
we like, but where He drives—rather say, where He *guides* us.

" Christ is coming, coming for you ; and when He comes He
will have so many people about Him, and an ' innumerable
company of angels.' But when you just catch sight of Jesus
coming, you will be ' caught up ' to meet Him, and you may say,
as a dear friend said at a Conference in Melbourne, ' Stand by,
angels and archangels ; stand by, cherubim and seraphim ; here

is a poor sinner who wants to see the Saviour who died for him ; '
and that will be just rapture."

The following year, 1879, was opened by a sermon on Sunday
morning by the Rev. J. C. Ryle on Ezekiel xxxvi. 26, " I will
take away the stony heart out of your flesh, and I will give
you a heart of flesh."

The Monday evening Prayer Meeting was addressed by the
Rev. H Webb-Peploe, who again spoke the next morning on
Elijah on Mount Carmel.

Canon Battersby in his opening address sounded a note of
Praise, a note of Adoration, and a note of Warning. The
early Prayer Meetings, as in the previous year, were, as far as
the address was concerned, entrusted to one speaker, and the
speaker chosen on this occasion was Pastor Otto Stockmeyer.
It was our privilege to see a good deal of both the Canon and
the Pastor at a Conference of the Evangelical Alliance in Basle.

The Pastor was my guest ; our beds were in the same room.
About five each morning—I was supposed to be asleep—I
heard my friend calling upon God and reading His Word.
Somewhat to my surprise it was the English Bible that he used,
But the fervour of his communion with his Heavenly King was
what struck one most. The impression it made on my mind
was deeper than that of seeing at that Conference a young
English theologian said to have been lately brought to Christ—
he is now known to the world by the vagaries of his criticism—
his name is Canon Cheyne. The impression was deeper than
that made by an address—true it was in French—by the
already venerable theologian, the Preceptor of the Emperor
Frederick, Professor Godet. There was a wonderful scene
at a garden party given by M. Vischer-Sarassin. And there
was a united Communion Service in the Cathedral, when a
great crowd, of various nations, walked to the Communion table,
and there received (standing) the sacred elements from the
hands of four of the clergy in their black gowns. But none
of these scenes remain with me more vividly or graciously than
that early morning prayer meeting in which I was but a silent
listener.

Later on one met the Pastor at many Conventions, and
especially at those in Glasgow. The friends who ordered it, hit

F

upon a plan admirably suited to a teacher who had not quite conquered the difficulties of the English language, and who also was too much of a mystic for his thoughts to be quite accessible to large audiences. At Glasgow he was given continual opportunities of pouring forth his teaching to as many as could receive it in a separate and smaller hall.

It was this saint of God who spoke at the 7 o'clock prayer meetings at Keswick in 1879. He dwelt on the work of the Spirit. "His name is Comforter to His disciples. He is the Convicter for the world.

"How long will Christians invert the offices of the Spirit, and oblige Him to be more convincing than comforting! Yet I have a deep feeling in these days that He must be that, must convince of sin, the sin of unbelief.

It is because of this sin that so many Christians—looking back a day, a week, a year—have not this testimony that they have pleased God. These meetings cannot have the approval of our Father unless a week after, a month after, a year after, there be at least some who have learned by faith to please God ; not coming back next year telling of the power of Jesus, yet when asked if they have proved it in their lives, having to confess that they have not habitually pleased God, or had the presence of the Holy Ghost as Comforter."

Next day he spoke of the fear of dying to self, of leaving our life in the hands of God. "We read of God's working in us to will and to do. To will what ? To do what ? To become like-minded with Jesus who was obedient unto death. The Holy Ghost make us willing to be from morning to evening a living sacrifice on the altar of the holy God."

Quoting I Kings x. 8, "Happy are thy men, happy are these thy servants, that stand continually before thee, and hear thy wisdom." Mr. Stockmeyer exclaimed : "Do you think the people of Israel would not hearken when Solomon called one of them to come to his house and stand before him ? I will only add one word—' HERE *is a greater than Solomon.*' "

On Saturday he pointed out that as it is said the Lord is Almighty, so it is said that faith is almighty (Matt xix. 26 ; Mark ix. 23), and in the same address he said, "Hell is self. Heaven is love." But he harked back to the other thought in closing, " Believe me, the devil cannot touch the strength of Jesus Christ."

On the last *evening* his message was " Go in peace " (2 Kings v. 19). " So do you go home, and at home you shall have direction from above for the day. Be not troubled beforehand. Perhaps the same God who has been working with *you* here, has been working with your beloved ones at home. But if not, when you go home cleansed, renewed, and at rest in Jesus, being in the hands of your Divine Guide, in any difficulty be not troubled. Jehovah will bring you through, but not telling you beforehand how He will do it. The little maiden *here* went into captivity *with Jehovah*, and brought to Syria the news that in Canaan there was a man that could cleanse lepers. That at the beginning. Then think of the end of the chapter, take the comparison between this maiden and Gehazi. He had lived in fellowship with the holiest man under heaven. But what a dreadful end he had—the leprosy of Naaman— because he was not single-hearted. It is of no use to be with Elisha, so long as you seek your own life."

A most notable figure appeared at Keswick, for the first time, in this year 1879—the Rev. Charles Armstrong Fox. "The very sight of him was a joy, and the sound of his voice an inspiration. Thoughts of him at Mildmay and Keswick, in his Church-room, and in private houses, come back like the melody of a well-tuned harp. He was like Mr. Great-Heart. For one thing he helped the pilgrims ; many a limping, halting soul is less lame to-day for his helpfulness." There is an exuberant, exquisite wealth of loveliness ; pile upon pile—in nature, in the Gospel, and in the setting forth of the Gospel by such men as he. You could never anticipate him. As well talk of anticipating the bend of a river, or the course of a comet. You never knew whether he would take you " to the third heaven or to the seventh " ; but wherever he took you, you knew (as we heard Mr. Bowker say to Mr. Fox one day) that you " would like to follow." " Was it not a great thing that it was shown in him that this Movement not only appealed to one class of mind ? Here was a born preacher, a born poet, too, become an exponent of it ? Ay, and what an exponent ? Those who only heard Mr. Fox in later years can be hardly conscious of the work he did twenty or thirty years ago. Every night *then* we looked for him, and every night he came, full of the Holy Ghost and of power, with deep thoughts and burning words to teach, and bruise, and heal, and build us up in Christ Jesus." These words kindly inserted in the Memorials of Mr. Fox, seem not less but more true to-day. " He was a beautiful friend ; as full of cheerfulness as of sympathy, and with an appositeness in all he said which was quite his own." After the baptism of her little one he wrote to an old friend :—

" I want desperately to see you and that prodigy of a boy, and that perfection of a husband, and that well-tried and well-beloved sister-friend of yours, Emma Waithman.

> " Father, mother, hasten home
> With thy living, latest treasure,
> Ere his spirit learn to roam,
> Or has tasted pain or pleasure ;
> Will him over, soul and limb,
> To the Lord in search of him ;
> Lay thy dedicated thing
> In thy Saviour's Hands, and sing !
> He who died to set him free,
> He will give him back to thee,
> Freely give, if freely given—
> Sealed with the Kiss of Heaven."

> Your loving Friend.
> CHARLES A. FOX."

That letter and those lines were written to one jubilant with joy, but he could touch the chord of sorrow with equal skill—

> " Ah, He knoweth ; ah, He loveth !
> Master, never let me go !
> Every wound Thy skill fresh proveth,
> Every cloud conceals Thy bow."

Being shown this during the days of agony preceding his death, the poet's pen wrote once more :—

> " Yes, to-day needs nothing newer,
> This brief record burns like fire ;
> Old truth but flames forth the truer,
> As He draws still nigher, nigher—
> Sweet His whisper, Come and rest,
> Wrecked outright on Jesus' breast ! "

Like the Church of the Testimony at Geneva, in which Cæsar Milan ministered, Eaton Chapel has been ruthlessly pulled down, but the voice that sounded there will never cease to vibrate—it sounds now in heaven.

This was the man whom Canon Battersby wooed from the South to the North of England for the Convention of 1879, and who for a quarter of a century from that time reached thousands of hearts at St. John's and in the tent. A few words from his address that year must close this chapter.

"The Master is come and calleth for thee," was his text. Having sketched the POWER of the Master, he touched on His WILL. There was the 'I will' of cleansing to the leper. The remarkable 'I will' in Matthew xx. 15. 'Is it not lawful for me to do what I will with mine own?' How blessed to be called His 'own'! I beseech you yield to it. I beseech you, *be at the mercy of Jesus*! The third 'I will' is to Peter—'If I will that he tarry.' How long you live how soon you die, is entirely at My disposal. Thus the 'I will' touches every circumstance. Yes, the 'I will' of Christ covers the whole of the Christian life. Is there more? 'Father, I will that they also whom Thou hast given Me be with Me where I am.' He came to where you were, and now, Lord, dost Thou raise us to be where Thou art! Just before He died, He made an inventory of all He had, and then gave it all away. 'My PEACE I give unto you.' 'That my JOY might remain in you." His 'BODY given for you.' His BLOOD shed for you. And twice He repeats another legacy. 'I have given them Thy WORD'—'The words which Thou gavest Me.' All He had He gave away. 'The GLORY which Thou gavest Me I have given them.' When He was on the cross—for He was never so rich as then—He gives away PARDON. He gives HOME, linking two of His own together for ever. There are no such friendships as those made at the Cross of Christ! He gives away PARADISE. 'To-day'—immediate transition when you take Christ! His very clothing was given away. 'They parted My garments among them.' 'They cast lots for HIS VESTURE.' I wonder what that soldier thought as He put on that seamless vesture : picture of us murderers clothed in the stainless robe of the righteousness of Christ.

"'The Master is come and calleth for THEE!' May I not

present you now with myself to Him as ' living sacrifices ' ?

" Oh, living, loving Saviour, we present unto Thee our bodies, our souls, our all ; we hold not one thing back, but as the woman cast in ' all her living,' we offer ourselves as living sacrifices on Thee, the Living Altar."

CHAPTER VIII

A MESSAGE FROM A SON OF FRANCE; A SONG FROM A DAUGHTER OF AFRICA

> " My Father is rich in houses and lands,
> He holds all the wealth of the worlds in His hands,
> Of rubies and diamonds, of silver and gold,
> His coffers are full, He hath riches untold.
> > I'm the child of a King,
> > The child of a King,
> With Jesus my Saviour, I'm the child of a King."
> > > > *Sung at Keswick*, 1881.

FEW men have touched the inner springs of this Movement more powerfully than the Rev. E. W. Moore. His chief influence was in London, and there and everywhere there was felt the power of stillness, the power of holiness. The crucifixion of the flesh, and the life in the Spirit, made and make this minister of Christ a ministering angel to very many. He gave the name to *The Pathway of Power* and again to *The Life of Faith*. He was the mainspring of a memorable Convention in Lancaster Gate in the early days, and of many such in Wimbledon, since he resided there. Testimonies to his goodness come from opposite quarters.

A retired Congregational minister in Essex loved to tell how, at a farewell meeting for our friend, who had been curate of the parish, after thanking the vicar, wardens, and others, Mr. Moore turned to this minister and said : " And there is another whom I must thank. I feel that I owe much, in girding on the harness, to the wise counsel of this elder brother in Christ who may be about putting if off." When incumbent of Brunswick Chapel, it was laid upon our friend's heart to hold holiness meetings, also to permit the prayers of some of our sisters. As he had no church room, the meetings were held in the church, and thus gave greater offence to some; so much so, that the matter was brought before Dr. Temple, then Bishop of London. He sent for Mr. Moore and asked him what holiness meetings were. One can imagine the description that was given of them. Then the fact that women prayed was touched upon. " It might be more prudent to omit *that,*" was the Bishop's comment, " but as to the holiness meetings I can imagine few things more profitable." Then turning to another subject, the Bishop asked Mr. Moore, " Do you think I am a converted man ? I have an old Methodist relative who thinks I am not ; but all I can say is that I do try to regulate my life to please my Lord."

At Wimbledon a remarkable tribute has been paid to Mr. Moore by the vicar of the parish, said to be a somewhat high churchman. He offered the incumbent of Emmanuel the privilege of appointment to a new district, future appointments to lie with Evangelical trustees. Of course there was a church to be built to cost many thousands, but, when four persons came forward with a thousand each, there was no difficulty on that score, and it was Mr. Moore's joy thus to bring to Wimbledon that valiant soldier of the Cross the Rev. G. Buchanan, now, to Wimbledon's loss, removed to Hull.

At Keswick our friend's voice was often heard speaking from the platform with addresses indicative of thorough preparation, exquisite literary taste, and above all deep spirituality. In quieter meetings, some of them not even on the programme, his peculiar powers had also play, and many felt that such meetings—freshets to fill the river—were worth all the other assemblies.

An earlier page tells how—was it not at Curzon Chapel in 1873 ?—our friend first drank of these deeper waters. But he has also often referred to a subsequent occasion—was it not in Exeter Hall ?—when from the lips of one blessed to multitudes, Catherine Booth, " Mother of the Salvation Army," he heard words that led to a deeper death with Christ, and a fuller life in the Spirit.

Another clergyman, well known in the early years at Keswick, had the current of his thoughts changed by the same remarkable woman. This was the Rev. J. A. Jacob, an Irish clergyman, but then having a church in London, and said to hold Broad church views ; but from this time Christ and His work shone before him with overwhelming power. It was good to see one whose mental horizon had been cold and grey, now gazing with fixed intent on the blood-red Sun of Righteousness. Year after year to him was entrusted the sifting of the sheaf of petitions for prayer. On a later day, in the city of Gloucester, we heard him give his testimony with humble frankness, and preside over an after meeting with impressive solemnity.

But to return to Mr. Moore, he had visited Keswick on a previous occasion, but the first address of his fully reported is in 1880. "I shall be anointed with fresh oil" (Psalm xcii. 10). "How we love fresh things. The world came fresh from the hand of the Creator. The worldling takes pains to obtain new things ; but there is only one place where we can find real newness—*in Christ*. In Him 'all things are become new.' In Him we are always secure of finding freshness—a life of surprises from the unfoldings of God—days of heaven upon earth. This is *holy oil* (lxxxix. 20). It is a solemn, an awfully solemn thing to come to a Convention for holiness ! Take care of unreal sanctification. Assure yourself that your anointing is real, and do not deceive yourself by any substitute for it. It is the anointing oil that secures love. If it is falling on us and on all our brethren, then we shall know how to love them. All one in the unity of the Spirit, we must love, we cannot help it ; we shall not be frozen, but melted into one.

"It is a *gladdening oil*. Christ's presence is not really rejoiced in without it. There must be a distinct work of the Holy Ghost. Self in the dust really surrendered ; then you have an indwelling Christ. When yielded right up to the Spirit He guides, but it costs us our will. It is because we do not go down into the place of death that we have not this *invigorating oil*. We say we are weak, but we do not get low enough ; we cannot share God's strength, but exchange our's for it."

We have said nothing about the Christian women to whom the Convention owed not a little. Indeed it is difficult to say much about them, because for the most part their meetings were to themselves, and the reports of these, specially in those early days, were exceedingly scanty. But we are sure that a great share of the blessing of Keswick is due to this hidden ministry. Who can doubt it that knows, for instance, Mrs. Michael Baxter, Mrs. Hopkins, Mrs. Penn-Lewis, Mrs. Bannister, or Miss Nugent and Miss Bradshaw?

But there were other Christian women whose names appear in the list of Conventions on each side of the year 1880. There came across the Atlantic the authoress of *Fulness of Blessing* and *Garden Graith*, Miss Sarah Smiley. Across the Atlantic also came a very different but equally impressive speaker who was at the Convention of 1881. This was Amanda Smith. "In her own thrilling, touching way," says the report, "she told how the Lord had led her on from blessing to blessing, giving her gradually more and more light as she was able to bear it. Her simple speech was so clothed upon by the power of the Holy Ghost, that hearts were melted, and the presence of that Near One seemed ever more intensely near, as she spoke of Him and the things she had seen and heard." People who heard her sing "I'm the child of a King" (p. 79) were so thrilled that they never forgot it.

A novel feature of that year was a Bible Reading at 9.45 a.m. The first to take it was Mr. Bowker. On the other three days the readings were given by the Rev. Hubert Brooke. We have always said that Mr. Bowker "discovered" Mr. Brooke, but we did not remember that he so literally introduced him to the Keswick gatherings, or that our friend, so specially identified with Bible Readings in many places, was, except for that one day, the first to initiate that means of grace at the great Convention. It is difficult to say what one would like to say of one who was for more than twelve years a neighbour, and for twice twelve years a friend. But surely there never was any one more eminently the right man in the right place than Mr. Brooke at a Bible Reading! His style, clear as a frosty night and bright as its stars, as full of vivacity as of solemnity, exactly suited the light touch of topic after topic from page to page, and book to book, of the wonderful Word of God. His argument, so forcible that it holds you in its grip, and his illustration so sunny that it attracts you by its radiance, must have made some of his hearers feel—I never knew there was so much in the Bible.

1882, the eighth year of the Convention, was indeed a "year

of the right hand of the Most High." The very invitation to it was couched in heart-stirring language. "The song of triumph and the shout of praise are much more heard, thank God, in the ranks of Christ's soldiery than in any times past which we can remember."

How the numbers attending were increasing is indicated by the suggestion for "early application for accommodation, as it is expected that there will be large demands upon the limited resources of the town." Almost a new town has grown up round the Tent in the generation following.

When the assembly gathered, Canon Battersby welcomed all who had come "for new, fresh blessing from the hand of God, and that we may *be* a blessing." That was on the Monday. Then on the Friday he referred to the Oxford Convention in these memorable words : "I got a revelation of Christ to my soul so extraordinary, so glorious, so precious, that from that day it illuminated my life. I found HE was *all* I wanted ; I shall never forget it ; the day and hour are present with me. How it humbled me, and yet what peace it brought ! Since then I have had opportunity for eight years to prove what is in Christ, and whenever I have trusted Him, I have always found Him faithful. I have never been disappointed in Christ. Whenever I have trusted Him with a full and entire trust, I have found Him all I needed. That is all I will say about myself. But I think it is important it should be known that it is not anything of our own we have discovered, or any definite *thing* we have got, but Christ Himself." These words—they recall Miss Havergal's sentence in *Such a Blessing*, "It lit up my life "—were enough to signalize the tent meetings, and when it is remembered that they were amongst the last this saint of God ever uttered under its sacred folds, it will be felt that they were God-given words indeed.

Those of whom we have spoken above had also messages from the Master for His servants.

In an address from Malachi iii. 2–4, on " Christ, the purging fire," the Rev. E. W. Moore asked, " How is this work of purifying to be carried on ? I believe," he answered, " there comes a time in the soul's history when it sees the Face of God in His holiness, and when it has held up before it an awful vision of selfishness at the root of much that appeared to be

Christian zeal. . . . It is always a sifting-time when Christ comes, a time of the exposure of shams. Some of us could witness that He suddenly comes to His Temple, and He comes with a cleansing fire."

Mr. Brooke referred to the fire also. " Look at the thorn tree in Exodus iii. 2, where ' the angel of the Lord appeared in a flame of fire out of the midst of the bush.' It is often taken as a type of the Church in the fire of affliction ; but that is not the real lesson, but that ' the Light of Israel shall be for a fire, and His Holy One for a flame.' These worthless bushes, with the Lord in the midst of them, can consume their enemies. We must learn these two lessons, that we are nothing but thorn bushes, and that the Lord is dwelling in us."

Mr. Fox spoke from " I will go and return to my place, until they acknowledge their offence, and seek My face " (Hos. v. 15). " If you want to have God's presence, there must be *confession. Confession is the instinctive speech of a broken heart, a heart crushed between the justice and mercy of God.* Go home to your room, and, there staring at you in the dark, you are aware of what sin hinders you. You know it well, and that it still clings, yet you will not renounce it. Come and acknowledge your offence. Break up the floor beneath your feet, and bring out whatever gold or Babylonish garment is hidden there. It is not hid from God. ' Get thee up ; wherefore liest thou thus upon thy face ? ' Stern words these to His blessed servant Joshua, words equivalent to ' I do not want prayer now.' There is a stain, sin must be forsaken. God is not with you because of it. Bring out the idol and place it at His feet, and break it there for ever.

" When Napoleon wanted to find where the dungeons of torture were in the Inquisition, he at last stood at a certain spot and said, ' Bring water.' They poured it over the floor, and where it ran down between the stones he said, ' Take up that stone.' There was the dungeon door, the place of torture. So God stands over against your sin. Let the water of the Word search it out, then give it up into the wounded hands of Jesus. Here all round, you see others getting blessing. Only ' acknowledge your offence,' He says ; He will go ' until ' you do, leaving His presence at your disposal."

Mr. Webb-Peploe : " All things are yours." " Claim it,

my brother, not as a promise, but as a fact, true of every child of God; first, a perfect position in Christ Jesus our Lord; next, a present donation of the Holy Ghost; and then, a present realization of all this. In 1 Corinthians vi. 19, St. Paul says, ' Ye are not your own.' The unsearchable riches of Christ mine, and yet I cannot call even myself my own!"

"People take *things* from Christ, some gift, the Bible, life, they never realize that their life *is* Christ, not only *from* Christ. Dr. Candlish said grandly, 'I have nothing *from* Christ, but I have all things *in* Christ.' He gives us not *things*, He gives us *Himself*."

But the teaching that rung in most memories after that Convention, came from a voice new to Keswick, the voice of Theodore Monod. His great hymn—

"Oh, the bitter shame and sorrow,"

was the Marseillaise of the Movement, and with other hymns of his is still often sung. So eager were people to hear him, that when the editor of one of our religious papers was asked if he would send a reporter to Keswick, he answered, "If Pasteur Monod is coming, yes; otherwise, no." I am not sure that except at Broadlands, Oxford, and Brighton, it would be easy to indicate this unique charm. Yet two or three extracts may illustrate the freshness and force of his words. M. Monod spoke thus on TAKING: "You have asked for a blessing, you have expected it, you have kept back nothing, and yet you seem to yourselves to be still unblessed. It remains for you to *take*. ' This is the record that God hath given to us eternal life.' Take it as freely as it has been given. A ship has been wrecked, the waves are beating it to pieces, but here comes a life-boat through the surge, and the brave men, at the peril of their lives, reach the doomed vessel, and beckon the crew to jump into the boat. But how can I know, says one of those ready to perish, that they will receive me into that life-boat? If they did not intend to receive him would they have come for him? So with Him who came to seek and save that which was lost. . . . ' I counsel thee to *buy* of Me gold tried in the fire.' Why should He speak of buying when we have no money to buy? A shopkeeper would understand. You enter a store where a great variety of views of these lakes are to be found. You look them over, talk them over, go into ecstasies, pronounce them beautiful, admirable, exquisite—and move out without having *bought* anything. So with the treasures of Christ, we may gaze at them, admire them, desire them, talk and sing about them, and enjoy them, enjoy nice books and nice Conventions, but we part with nothing and obtain nothing. Will we now buy of Him who asks but our guilty, blind, naked, miserable selves, and offers Himself, the very brightness of the glory of God ? . . . How are we separated from sin ? By the death of Christ. ' If one died for all, then all died.' Then what have you to do in order to die to sin ? To take hold of that fact. To believe that Christ by His death has created a separation between you and your sin ; that the old man (that is, the man you used to be) is on Christ's cross, and that the new man in you is free to be used for God by His Spirit. We belong to Him, and all we have belongs to Him, and it is a perfect shame that we should take days and hours to decide whether He should have us or not."

" ' He shall call upon Me and I shall answer him.' A true prayer meeting will lead to an answer meeting. ' With long life will I satisfy him, and show him My salvation,'—show us at what cost we are saved. Do you think we know *that* ? Show us out of what we are saved, and into what we are saved, now and hereafter. Showing us means making us hunger and thirst for it, and then satisfying us, giving us no ' second blessing ' only, but blessing number three, and four, and five, and fifty, and a hundred, and a thousand."

CHAPTER IX

"GOD BURIES HIS WORKMEN, BUT CARRIES ON HIS WORK"

> " Thus he in meekness proved himself to be,
> Throughout long years of lowly ministry—
> (Bear witness, ye ungrudging Brotherhood
> Of kindred souls linked round his open grave !)
> One of God's mountain messengers of light,
> Whose feet stand on the mountains next the dawn,
> And who from misty valleys upward lure
> The fearful flock, and tempt to breezy heights
> And thymy pastures sweetened by the sun ! "
>
> C. A. Fox.

NO one who was at the Convention of 1883 can ever forget it. It was " enclosed in death. We have been invited to the feast," said the Rev. C. A. Fox, " and now the head of the house himself has left us and gone within. He is in the brighter light of the glory, and we are still in the shadow, but it is the shadow cast by Christ Himself."

Canon Harford-Battersby, stricken with illness inscrutable, " died on the morning of the day on which the Convention assembled," and was buried ere the Convention closed. The great concourse of people from the town and from the county was swollen to a vast assembly at the grave. The love of the departed towards all saints was not forgotten by the survivors, one of the pall-hearers being the Rev. Alfred Howson,[1] the Congregational minister of Keswick ; also one of the four preachers asked, in church or tent, to speak words to the living concerning him numbered with the blessed dead being the present writer. The others were Canon Richmond, Mr. Fox, and Mr. Hopkins.

[1] This good minister of Jesus Christ soon after fell asleep, and his grave is the nearest to the Canon's in St. John's Churchyard.

At the grave the vast assembly listened to words of deep solemnity from Preb. Webb-Peploe.

Another day, Mr. Fox said : "The circumstances of the funeral are but the putting away of the poor clay clothes into the wardrobe of earth, whence they shall be brought forth transfigured into the likeness of HIS glorious body. . . . I saw him several times in London, and saw the perfect peace and sweet rest on his poor wasted face and wasted frame. Though knowing how ill he was and of the meetings where he could not be, there was still the same calm smile as if he were already in Heaven ; and indeed, as was said of another, ' he always lived so near Heaven that, when God called him, he had not far to go.' " "Of him it may be truly said," wrote H. F. B., "that no one was more fitted by the simplicity and purity of his life to take a prominent part in seeking to reawaken the Church of God to live the life of Christ."

Dr. Elder Cumming quotes in reference to him, " They saw his face, as it had been the face of an angel." The same thing had been said in rougher fashion by a fellow-student at Oxford : " If he was put into the dock in a court of justice on any charge, no jury would be found to convict, after they had seen his countenance."

Not even the greatness of our loss kept us from the high purpose of the Convention. The veterans wielded the sword of the Spirit with their accustomed power, and it was good to find others coming up to their side : The Revs. Colin Campbell, a beautiful embodiment of the meekness and gentleness of Christ ; J. Stephens, a coadjutor of Canon Hay Aitken, and Dr. Elder Cumming, who was destined to do great things for Scotland. At the closing meeting special solemnity attached to the words of Mr. Robert Wilson, the colleague in this noble work of the departed saint. " The Convention has now been held for nine years," he said, " and in all that time dear Canon Battersby and I had never one unsettled word, though we did help one another by difference of opinion. I knew the Lord would bless us this time again. I was sure He would not take the leader, and forget to come Himself. Last year our friend said, ' Mr. Wilson and I shall not be very long with you ' ; but I little thought that he was to be taken and I left. Pray for me, that if the Lord will He may prepare us to meet again."

The speaker did not say *where*. Moreover he did not act as chairman. In his modesty he had thrust that honour on Mr. Bowker, " a man of great vigour of mind, long at the head of one of the great schools of the country. A man of great private influence," as Dr. Cumming writes.

The same reminds us of his telling a story of his being in Lord Brougham's company. " A question arose as to what Great Britain owed her greatness to. Brougham evaded the question, and referred to Mr. Bowker, who answered : ' It is to her possession of the Word of God, in the English Bible.' Brougham bowed his head, and added : ' I should not wonder if you be correct ! ' "

Mr. Bowker doubted whether, as the vicar of the parish *might* no longer be a leader of the Convention, it would not be better to remove it from Keswick to some other place. He had an opportunity of putting his views before half a dozen or more of the speakers, for they happened to be in Brighton late in the year 1883. There was a Convention in the Dome and in the Pavilion, the leading spirit in the gatherings there was a Christian gentleman in broken health, the late Major Way. At his beautiful house, Wick Hall, some rare and heavenly meetings had been held in 1879. The Major was able to be present in a quiet corner of the great drawing-room, which was crowded in every part. The meeting, commenced by Canon Auriol with a reading of Scripture, was then thrown open for any to follow as God might lead in hymn, or prayer, or address. These were morning meetings. In the afternoon and evening, Dean Freemantle (the elder) and others presiding, the meetings were in the Dome. In 1883, Major Way, still more an invalid, could not be present, but there gathered in his dining-room a. little company on whose opinion seemed to depend the serious question of the continuance of the Convention at Keswick, or its removal elsewhere.

Mr. Bowker stated the view indicated. His opinion was felt to have much weight, for few men in England were more apt at rallying the forces of God's people. But Mr. Fox, Mr. Hopkins, and every one else who was present, urged that, God had so manifestly brought us to Keswick, that it would indicate want of faith to leave it. With this unanimous decision Mr. Bowker fell in, in the most chivalrous spirit, and

G

pressed forward the gathering of the clans at Keswick as if the proposal had been his own. With equal zest, he pressed forward other gatherings which, about this time, were signally owned and blessed of God in many parts of the land, and indeed beyond it,—for away in Australia, and by and by in other Colonies, Conventions were held.

Probably the most notable of such Conventions was that gathered in the city of Glasgow, due undoubtedly under God to the energy and devotion of Dr. Elder Cumming. " It was in the last and closing year of Canon Battersby's chairmanship at Keswick that I made his acquaintance," writes Dr. Cumming, " and paid my first visit to the Convention. I remember his sermon, and some of his short glowing words from the chair. I saw something of the home life at the vicarage, most of all I remember his face. No other face I have ever seen has expounded for me Acts vi. 15, but his did. During the same year (1882) I went to the small Convention at Polmont, where Mr. Bowker presided. We also held a large meeting at Glasgow, where Canon Battersby was present ; so that in Scotland the Movement was fairly begun, and had taken hold. In 1883 we gathered again at Keswick, the first year I spoke there ; but the news met us at the station on Monday that Canon Battersby had died that morning. What a shock it was ! What a sermon ! What a teaching, that this work was not to stand in the power or wisdom of men ! What a lesson, if we could learn it, that God was sufficient, and that God was alone ! And all through the Convention, over which dear Mr. Bowker was chairman, the shadow of the grave, dark, sad, but tender and impressive, was upon us all."

It would not be easy to over-estimate the influence of Dr. Cumming on his brother ministers of the Established Church of Scotland, and of other churches there. At his hospitable table we remember meeting Dr. Marshall Lang, later promoted to the Principalship of Aberdeen University, (he was the father of the Archbishop of York,) Dr. Charteris, the eminent Edinburgh Professor, and last but not least, a leader among Scotland's Free Churchmen, the saintly Dr. Andrew Bonar. His brother put his poetry into his hymns ; *he* put his poetry into the *Life of Murray McCheyne*, and into his preaching. Like many of the older Evangelicals, he was shy of " the Movement," but not too shy to come to the meetings, and, from the body of the hall, to hear what was taught. Next year he was amongst us on the platform, and the third year he was one of the speakers. So this work of God grew. The numbers multiplied, the Queen's Rooms gave place to the City Hall, and, one year at least, the City Hall to St. Andrew's Hall.

We hope we do not disparage the work of other Scotch clergymen, like the Rev. John Sloan—alas! that he and now a much younger man, the Rev. Hector Mackinnon, should have been called away from us!—when we repeat that a large share of the influence in Glasgow at that time was due to the work of Dr. Elder Cumming. This will not surprise those who time after time listened to his massive and masterly addresses. He was still more impressive when, speaking at Keswick two years later, he said: " We came to God saying, I know that my sins are taken away, but there are so many great and so many little sorrows in this daily life of mine. My Father, hast Thou no deep peace for the soul that looks to Thee ? And He answered, ' Thou wilt keep him in perfect peace,' etc. (Isa. xxvi. 3). Dear child of God, thou art bearing thine own care. Take the peace of Heaven—a promise and a gift. Then I was always making mistakes, and the cry of the heart was : O that I had somebody to guide me ! And God's answer came— ' I will guide thee with Mine eye.' Just what I was wanting. I did not think it was a real thing ; but now I have come to take God's every word for gospel. Then I feel that I need keeping ; never a day nor an hour but I need to be kept. ' Father, canst Thou condescend to be my Keeper ? Thou knowest how bad, how false, how foolish I have been many a time. I need this tongue to be kept, this inconstant heart, and these thoughts. But Thou art so busy, I cannot ask Thee to keep them.' But I turn to Philippians iv. 7 (R.V.), and I read, ' shall keep thy heart and thoughts.' Then as a child of God I cannot go on without something like victory in my life ! I dare not look Christ in the face unless I have victory over the old habits of sin. Well, Thy dear servant John tells me, ' This is the victory that overcometh the world, even our faith.' Then I must pray, Father, I have had so many things from Thee already, but I want the greatest of all—*Thyself*. I come to Conventions and hear speakers talking of blessings, but I cannot do without Thyself. Satisfy Thy child's heart. And He does, saying, 'I am continually with thee.' . . . Standing on this spot, Canon Battersby told us how at Oxford he lay awake, and during that night he had a sight of the glory of the Lord. He said he could not put it into words, but he never forgot it. Perhaps such a sight would enable us to step into the fullest blessedness of Christian experience here."

No wonder that a teacher like this had wonderful influence, especially in the land of his birth and ministry. Reports of the Glasgow Conventions fill almost as large a space in some volumes of *The Life of Faith* as those of Keswick. To make but one quotation. A minister of "the Evangelical Union," writing to a Glasgow paper, said : "Sitting among the hundreds of saved and consecrated souls ; looking on them, with their notebooks ; witnessing the eagerness with which they turn up passages in their Bibles ; kneeling with them, a thousand at once, upon our knees, consecrating ourselves to God in Christ ; listening to the testimonies of ministers and people cultured and noble-looking, as well as of servants and shop lads ; all speaking of the blessedness and power of abiding in Christ and Christ in them, my feelings and longings were unutterable. . . . Here is a Movement (surely from God) proclaiming emphatically, fulness of peace, fulness of love, fulness of purity, fulness of power for service.

" You are calling for a new departure. Oh, if it were possible for us to call for the brethren of the Deepening of Spiritual Life Movement—to lay aside for the week our ordinary routine of business, and sit in the silence of a deep sincerity as in God's presence, listening to their teachings, and appeals, in the Holy Ghost—the new departure, as I think, would soon be taken."

In speaking of Glasgow and its palmy days, we are not forgetting the Bridge of Allan and " days of heaven upon earth " there, where Dr. Ferguson, Mr. Moffat, Mr. McFarlane, Mr. Hector Mackinnon and many more kept the flag flying. But this was later on. Edinburgh itself has had memorable meetings, but not annually as in the other centres. There were times when some said that Scotland would outstrip England in the proclamation of these truths ; and, as we shall see, Ireland would by no means be left out. So a master workman might fall, but the work went on.

CHAPTER X

A CRY FROM MACEDONIA

" A cry, as of pain,
Again and again,
Is borne o'er the deserts and wide-spreading main :
A cry from the lands that in darkness are lying,
A cry from the hearts that in sorrow are sighing ;
It comes unto me ;
It comes unto thee ;
Oh what—oh what shall the answer be ? "

SARAH GERALDINA STOCK.

THE year 1885 was marked by the home-call of two sisters in Christ intimately associated with this Movement. " Since last year the Lord had taken home the dear wife of Mr. Robert Wilson, and now on the very eve of the meetings, to Mrs. Battersby," the Christiana of the Convention, came " a post from the Celestial City," with the words, " I bring thee tidings, that the Master calleth for thee, and expecteth that thou shouldst stand in His presence, in clothes of immortality, within ten days." The messenger gave her a token, " an arrow sharpened with love let easily into her heart. Then she called for her children, and gave them her blessing ; and told them that she had read with comfort the mark that was set in their foreheads, and was glad to see them there, and that they had kept their garments so white. She called for Mr. Valiant-for-truth, and said, Sir, you have showed yourself true-hearted ; be faithful unto death, and my King will give you a crown of life. She gave Mr. Stand-fast a ring. And when the day drew near that she must be gone, behold, all the banks beyond the river were full of horses and chariots to convey her to the city gate. She entered the river, with a beckon of farewell to those that followed her. The last words that she was heard to say were, I come, Lord, to be with Thee and bless Thee."

Bunyan's matchless description suits our sainted sister as aptly as his heroine. And how would the immortal dreamer have depicted the scene at the grave, when the earthly garb of this later Christiana was folded away in the same death chamber as that to which, two years before, the earthly vesture of her beloved husband was committed ! Almost the same throng, townsfolk, and Convention folk mingled, gathered in the beautiful churchyard, whence hundreds withdrew to the tent to listen to words that sought to use the pathos of the hour to help the souls of those that sorrowed, so far to anticipate *their* home-call that heaven might begin below.

A call of a very different kind came to Keswick the following year, 1886. It was the cry from Macedonia. A missionary meeting led by Mr. Reginald Radcliffe was not a mere addition but a part of the actual Convention. It was to have lasted only an hour, but we could not separate then, and it awoke a thrill of hope, that the distant, toiling, lonely missionaries might come in for a share of our spiritual blessing.

This was a new departure, and surely a most blessed one. It has linked the ends of the earth to Keswick. Moreover, it has proved that those who gather in our tents are not content to keep the good things to themselves. They have heard the word, " Go your way, eat the fat and drink the sweet, and send portions for those for whom nothing is prepared."

The details of the " Missionary Element " of the Movement are given so fully in Dr. Harford's volume,[1] that the best thing we can do is to refer our readers to those chapters, saying only this, that voices from India, from Africa, from China, Protestant missionaries of all the Churches, have, we trust, received, have, we know, contributed, blessed and beautiful gifts to the understanding and advancement of the spiritual life by their introduction to the Keswick Movement. And who can forget appeals of Bishop Tucker, in St. John's Church, of Bishop Cassels, Bishop Peel, Bishop Tugwell ? Who can forget Miss Amy Wilson-Carmichael's farewell address, ere she left for her life of sacrifice in India, as she unrolled a " ribband of blue "

---

[1] *The Keswick Convention ; Its Message, Its Method, and Its Men.*

with the golden words, " Nothing too precious for Jesus " ? Who could ever forget, if they had had the privilege accorded to some of us, of being present at the missionary welcome meeting, or at a more private missionary farewell meeting, when round the supper table they gave one another parting texts to cheer them on their journeys to distant and difficult lands ?

" The first address in this country of Mr. R. P. Wilder, who had come to start the Students' Volunteer Movement, was given at the Saturday Missionary Meeting of 1891." And some of us who heard that address felt it to be epoch-making, as the rallying of young men to that standard has fully proved. It was in 1888 that an envelope was sent up to the chairman of the Missionary Meeting " containing £10 offered as ' the nucleus of a fund for sending out a Keswick missionary.' There had been no intention to have a collection, but within the next hour money and promises came up spontaneously, amounting to about £150. Before the end of the year the sum reached £908 for ' the Keswick Mission Fund,' besides £151 for existing Missionary Societies.

" The first to be sent forth was the Rev. George Grubb, and the result was the remarkable series of Missions conducted by him and his friends in Ceylon, South India, Australia, and New Zealand. Subsequently, the Revs. Hubert Brooke, C. Inwood, and G. H. C. Macgregor went to Canada on a similar errand ; and year by year since, others have gone forth. Mr. Inwood especially has done great service in South Africa, South America and the West Indies." [1] There are few more gracious names on the Keswick list than that to which Dr. Stock so suitably refers. We who well know Mr. Inwood in his own home and ours, who have listened to him from Keswick platforms and Brighton pulpits,.thank God with all our hearts for using him here, and for great good wrought by him amongst scattered Christian workers, converts lately won to the Saviour, and heathen people on whom as well as others deep solemnity fell as he proclaimed the love of God and the grace of our Lord Jesus Christ.

Brethren *from* the mission field must also have a word of notice. The presence of Hudson Taylor on the list of speakers for 1887 " showed that there was a conviction that consecration

[1] Abridged from Dr. Harford's volume.

included the missionary claim." Was it that year that he startled us (though it was just like him), by saying, " We have just been singing—

> ' They who trust Him wholly,
> Find Him wholly true.'

Yes, and I have proved that sometimes though we do not trust Him wholly, yet we find Him wholly true ? "

Another day, quoting Zephaniah iii. 15, " The King of Israel, even the Lord, is in the midst of thee, thou shalt not see evil any more." " This sweeps away," he said, " every thought that ' my experience is against it.' It says, What is your experience worth ? If I were to say to a Chinaman who had never seen a railway, ' I shall take you along at the rate of thirty miles an hour,' he would say, ' All my experience is against it ' ; would that make it untrue ? And God says, ' Thou shalt not see evil any more.' We are going to be carried along in His will, and we are not going to walk any more on our own feet."

Another witness for Christ from another Eastern Land was heard that year in the tent. This was Mr. Gelson Gregson, who wielded in England for some years a power like that he wielded amongst British soldiers in India. He spoke " of Christ as King." " Five years ago a friend of mine was here and found Christ to be his King. That message brought to me at Mussoorie, brought me to Keswick. I went on fencing and resisting, but when the Lord brought home the truth to me, I went straight to God and said, ' Lord, that man has a rest that I know nothing about, a peace which to me has been a dream, and he talks to me about " crossing Jordan," a thing I only expected to do when I die ; he says I must do it now.' I did not understand it, and I told the Lord so. He showed me that the throne of my heart was occupied, and I did not know it. We may as well be straight about this matter. The reason you do not surrender is fear of consequences ; you will have to give up something, and are not quite satisfied as to what God is going to do with you. But you cannot have this rest until you are in His hand. Some people keep themselves good by suppression. God does better ; He takes away the evil desire ; then when the devil puts the bait in front of you, you don't jump at it like a trout, because there is no desire to have it. You have argued and argued against it. Stop arguing, and let the Lord put you upon the wheel. Let His hand turn that wheel, and His fingers mould you into a vessel meet for the Master's use."

This " cry from Macedonia " would be quite incomplete without reference to the immense impetus given by Dr. Eugene Stock. His interest in the Movement ought to be read—and re-read—in the pages of his great book, *The History of the Church Missionary Society*. But others of us have a mental record more personal. We recall him as a chairman of infinite resource, not excluding humour, both at the Missionary Meetings duly scheduled in the programme, and at meetings not appearing in print, but delightfully carried out on some islet in the Lake. In private too Dr. Stock was full of *verve*, keen alike for the work of missions and for the main purpose of the Convention.

CHAPTER XI

" A TRUE WITNESS DELIVERETH SOULS "

" ' And there He blessed him.' The same hand that smote
Now blessed ; for all who touch the lowest hem
Find in the dust access to Deity."

THE six years of Mr. Bowker's presidency were years of progress both extensively and intensively. Not that Canon Battersby was forgotten, but, while the disciple was taken, the Lord was left, and He did " great things for us whereof we are glad."

The prevailing thought in the year 1884 was that of the Holiness of God, in 1885 that of our Humiliation.

The next year has inscribed upon it, " It was deeper progress through the valley all the way."

In 1888 the same pen writes " Great rain and great blessing," " worth coming from Kamschatka for," a business man said.

As to numbers, the year after we lost our leader there was a larger attendance than ever. The new Tent was packed to overflowing, and many stood outside. On one day 600 came from Barrow, quickened by the successful ministry of the Rev. W. Laycock. In 1885 " the large tent could not hold the increased numbers, and there were rows of seats on the grass outside." In 1886 the tent had been made twenty feet longer. It was still too small. The number of new faces was remarkable, clergymen and noted workers who had held rather aloof were here this time. Ireland sent a greatly enlarged band both of clergy and laity ; Scotland was fully represented ; and there never had been so many missionaries. Another feature was the grand band of *young* servants of God from Universities and elsewhere, and of maidens eager to learn a deeper devotion. So striking was the number of men that it was considered by

one on the platform that there were more of them than women.
In one gathering for young men only, the Lecture Hall was
crowded. It was led by Dr. Elder Cumming, and was filled
with solemn awe and humbling power. Many moving con-
fession-prayers broke out. A clergyman present remarked
that he had never been at such a meeting before, and had
never thought such an one were possible.

The next year there were more than ever to test the fulness
of blessing—a pentecostal three thousand. Villages round
Keswick had to receive guests. One house was filled by
eighteen men, gathered by two brothers converted at the Convention a year before. There were eighty-nine present at a
special communion for ministers on Friday morning, by the
invitation of the Vicar, the Rev. J. N. Hore.

The following year one note of number is recorded. "Throughout the Sunday that crowned the Convention 738 partook
[at St. John's] of the feast which is a consecration of spirit,
soul, and body, to Him who hath given all for us."

In each of these years interesting reference is made to the
Ladies' Meetings conducted by Mrs. Bannister, Mrs. Hopkins,
Mrs. Tottenham, and Miss Nugent, whose hand we trace in
most of the records of this period. But in the year 1889
evidently another chronicler took her place, and what is lost
in one way is gained in another, for there is an account, all too
brief, of one of Miss Nugent's addresses. "After full surrender,"
she said "after yielding to God to work His will in us, He
makes strong in the weakest places." From the keynote
"The lame take the prey," and "they that stumbled are
girded with strength," it was shown how incessantly God
pledges Himself not only to build anew, but to do it on the
desolated spots; so that "the land which had been as the
wilderness might become as the Garden of Eden."

The more we dive into Keswick records the more pearls we
find. Take this from Theodore Monod—"A man has a bad
tooth, and it has to be pulled out. He makes a great ado
about it. He would rather have a talk with the dentist about
dentistry among the ancients, or dentistry in general, or about
his own tooth—how bad it is and so forth. But when it comes
to having it out—oh! that is a different matter. So we
talk about sin, and about sinning and about freedom from sin.

People say it is so nice, oh ! so nice ; but when it comes to having it out, it is not so very nice ! And yet that is a part of salvation ; to have the power of sin broken." Take this of the Rev. Colin Campbell—" Is it exaggeration to say that though eighteen hundred years have passed since Christ said ' Ye shall receive power,' yet the Church is still a congregation of impotent folk ? " This of Mr. Webb Peploe's—" I thought, said a friend to me, you taught the eradication of sin. God forbid, I said, *You* preach a perfect sinner, *I* preach a perfect Saviour." That was at the close of a deeply solemn address on SIN. The following morning the same speaker took GRACE for his subject, and in dealing with it said these precious words : " I believe there is not a single wrong desire of the heart which may not be completely quenched by the Grace of God, I believe that He is able so to put forward the blessed Lord Jesus, so to exhibit the beauty of the Saviour, so to attract the heart and will, and the feelings of a man, that he can look up into the face of the Lord Jesus as the sweetest and all absorbing thing ; so that the man has no room for naughty appetite or desire."

One of the notable utterances of these years was that of the Rev. George Grubb, from the incident of David's longing for water of Bethlehem (2 Sam. xxiii. 15–17). " I am deeply anxious that every one of you should have such a loyal heart as to be willing to go through the opposing host of the Philistines to try and get a cup of cold water for Jesus, to satisfy the terrible thirst that is upon His soul. A great thirst lies upon the soul of Emmanuel. Does the blessing you profess to have received result in soul-thirst ? Has the salvation of the world ever cost you one single tear in your prayers ? Have you ever lain in agony before God, because the whole world lieth in' the wicked one ? Have you sympathy with Christ, or are you still going to give Him a draught of vinegar ? He has had enough of that already, and He would like a cup of pure cold water from you now." . . . " A great many Christians are suffering from weak action of the heart towards the Lord Jesus ; and that is a very dangerous thing. Yes, many Christians have heart-disease, and do not know it.

" Many say to me, I feel the want of God's love and know not how to get it. I will tell you how. ' Therefore doth my Father

love me because I lay down my life for the sheep.' When you
have laid down your life at the feet of God, you will know
that you have done it ; and when the deed is done—not when
you *pretend* to do it—then the love of the Father will come in,
and flood your soul. Theories about holiness will be explained
in having the reality." " If this Convention is to be a blessing
we must learn the secret of Fellowship. Then with a single
eye to my glorified and once crucified Saviour, His smallest
wish becomes law to me. I will dart off, as did the mighty
three, in the alacrity of faith, to do His holy will ; and the
chariots and horses of fire will be round me to protect me from
the hosts of the Philistines. Though you may be scarred and
wounded in the battle—your life-blood poured forth—you will
bring your gift to the feet of your David and give it to Him,
and He will in His turn pour it out to Jehovah."

At this Convention Mr. Brooke returned after three years
of enforced absence. " I spent last winter," he said " in a
place as high as one can be in winter, 6,000 feet above the sea.
As you go up every 1,000 feet, the pocket-barometer, set for
sea-level, goes down one inch. Thus as self goes down, the
soul goes up ; the nearer to the Lord, the farther from the
earth. The barometer had gone down past change, and rain,
and much rain, and storm, and had left them all behind for
perpetual sunshine. God can take us up there, if we are willing
to go down thus."

The next time some of us heard Mr. Brooke's voice was at
the funeral of Mr. Bowker. The latter had had a stroke in the
early part of that year, and had lost his speech, but he came
to Keswick and even presided at the meetings. It was a
pathetic sight to see him occupying his accustomed place, but
to hear his messages only through the lips of others. A few
weeks afterwards " God's hand smote him and he slept,"
passing from the silence of earth to join in the songs of heaven.
We laid him in the grave at Norwood Cemetery. Mr. Brooke,
as has been said, conducted the service. Mr. Wilson, on whom
the mantle and the burden of the departed chairman were now
to fall, travelled all the way from Cumberland to stand by the
grave of his friend. A minister, once a scholar at Christ's
Hospital, where Mr. Bowker long held an important post, writes
to us, " I am able to say that what led Mr. Bowker, under

the guidance of the Holy Spirit, towards the Keswick movement was a growing conviction that God meant His people to enjoy a higher, brighter and more conquering life and experience than Christians at that time enjoyed, or, indeed, knew anything about. There was first the personal hunger, then, the persuasion, the realization of the possibility of a much higher attainment in the divine life, and then, under the teaching of the Word and by prayer, he entered into rest of soul and joy in God by faith."

The Chairman of the Council, the Rev. Evan Hopkins, regarded Mr. Bowker's adhesion to the movement as an event of no small importance ; assuredly he manifested an organizing faculty beyond all the rest of our leaders.

Till the resurrection morning his mortal remains sleep, not far from those of the great pastor and preacher, Charles Haddon Spurgeon.

CHAPTER XII

RIGHTEOUSNESS AND REST

" In Keswick Vale, see fair July,
  With glory lights the earth and sky,
    And hill and grove and winding stream,
    Adorned in summer beauty, seem
  The reflex of a world on high.

" Tis sweet to gaze with raptured eye
  On Derwent's placid bosom nigh,
  On verdant slope to bask and dream
    In Keswick Vale.

" But here in Peniel Shade hard by
  Are truer joys for which we sigh,
    Christ Saves and Keeps : we hear the theme,
    That floods our hearts with bliss supreme,
  And secret Care and Unrest die
    In Keswick Vale."

From *Keswick Vale and Other Poems,* by S. M'CURRY.

MR. WILSON taking up his work in the year 1890 read words from Haggai (ii. 5.) an encouragement to himself and the people, " My Spirit remaineth among you, fear ye not." It so happened that we met on the seventh month, the one and twentieth day of the month, which made the quotation the more appropriate. Later on he exclaimed : " Brethren, pray for us. Do. We greatly need it."

The *British Weekly* wrote : " The Keswick Convention is a great institution, it is so in the numbers attending it from all parts of the world, in the infectious enthusiasm which marks all its meetings, and above all in the potent influence it is exerting. The numbers present, especially clergymen, are simply astonishing. The picturesque little town is crowded to overflow with those who come, six or seven hours a day listening to prayers or addresses. Nothing has more surprised me," adds the writer, " than the eagerness with which the vast audience followed the speakers in their expositions of the Bible, following them in the Book and taking down the substance of the addresses. What is peculiar to Keswick is that emphasis is given to some aspects of evangelical truth largely neglected. Greater stress is laid on the certainty of victory over sin, through faith in the power of an indwelling Saviour. Yet speaker after speaker disclaimed all sympathy with the doctrine of sinless perfection. Confessions of sin and unworthiness were frequent, yet there was also what Thomas Carlyle calls ' The killing of self which is,' he says, ' and ever will be, the beginning of all real worth and work under the sun.' Special emphasis is also attached to the waiting upon God in faith in order to be filled with the Holy Spirit." E. R. B. (we have no idea whom these initials represent) closes this record " by repeating that Keswick Convention is a great institution, and it will be a thousand pities if our Nonconformist leaders withhold from it their sympathy and support."

The attendance this year again increased. Trains had to come in detachments, every lodging was full, and a camp also.

Amongst those who came for the first time was Miss Marsh, in 1913 laid in her honoured grave. Mr. Grubb and his companions came in the middle of the week and told of their wonderful journey in Ceylon, in New Zealand and other places. The next year they were welcomed in Australia, and that visit is described by *The Times* as having " evoked an extraordinary exhibition of religious fervour at Geelong. Mr. Grubb appealed for money in support of the Mission, and the people responded by giving their purses unopened, their watches and rings, while women stripped off their jewellery, and personal adornments. Others gave hastily-executed conveyances of land and other property. In a few minutes money and property valued at £1,500 had been subscribed."

The first address was by Dr. Cumming on Bethel ; the next by Preb. Webb-Peploe on Carmel. Mr. Fox, following in prayer, said " The fire has fallen, the rain is coming, link us all in one, round Thy altar, Jesus Christ. We are very near to Bethel, the gate of heaven, where he is who presided over us. Abase us, O God, if in any way we have arisen."

At one of the Ladies' Meetings a speaker said "Jewels need not fear the fire. Is not the reason for our fear that we know so much would be consumed that we want to keep ? "

Of that fire, or rather of that Holy Spirit, so many speakers spoke that it was said that the progress was not, as often, from

Passover to Pentecost, but from Pentecost to Passover. The Rev. Barclay Buxton preached on " Are ye able to be baptised with the baptism wherewith I am baptised ? " The Rev. Handley Moule preached on " Christ our passover is sacrificed for us." " The believer's life when he knows Christ as a sacrifice for him, should be the keeping of a feast. The discovery of this has made life a new thing to many of us."

At the Ministers Meeting Mr. Webb Peploe put the difference between the former teaching and this in a crisp sentence. " Before, I expected failure, and was astonished at deliverance ; now, I expect deliverance, and am astonished at failure." Dr. Cumming said " There will ever be a need of an accepting and an emptying, for a man living the life of the Spirit is not perfect, yet very different from the old man who had his name, his clothes, his shoes. All he may be able to tell you is :—it is not I but Christ." Dr. White, then of Winchester, speaking of discipleship and cross-bearing, closed with this bright illustration, " As one dear to me wrote, ' as I walk in and out among the children it is as if the Master walks side by side with me.' This is true, in your business, in your household and its cares, you will know that the Master is actually by your side. He wakeneth mine ear to hear as a disciple." Yes, this is true, but let us remember, as Mr. Gregson said, to use " the safeguard of eternal vigilance."

One of the texts taken by Dr. Cumming was—" And the disciples were filled with joy and the Holy Ghost." " Then," said he, " there is such a thing as the filling of disciples, of many disciples, of nameless disciples, with the Holy Ghost. And yet there are numbers of Christians who have never contemplated the possibility of having the Holy Ghost to fill them. He is willing to fill us on condition that we be emptied first. And what does this fulness mean ? Christ made precious in our eyes, the heart cleansed and the life purified, joy for our strength, peace for our keeping, power for our usefulness. Oh ! people of Keswick, shall there not rise from your hearts a united cry, a cry of faith, Lord fill me, fill me with the Holy Ghost on Thine own terms."

Dr. White, that good soldier of Jesus Christ, one morning reminded us of God's question to Adam " Where art thou ? " (Gen. iii. 9), and of the question of the wise men concerning

Christ " Where is He ? " (Matt. ii. 2). " Have you a consulta-
tion with the Master as to what to do, to speak, to write, to
think of, day by day ? Let us live and walk in His ceaseless
presence. And let me ask a third question. Have you seen
His star, are you looking for HIM ? What makes the day ? The
sun. What brings the sun ? The dawn. What ushers in the
dawn ? The day star. Has the Day Star risen in your hearts ?
Are we walking *with* the King, living *for* the King, dwelling so
really in the presence of the King, that if He were to come now
and take us home it would be but the passing from spiritual
sight to actual, of a Face long loved, and to see Whom in His
beauty we have daily yearned ? "

It was at this Convention (1891) that Theodore Monod
exclaimed " I sometimes think, looking at our flags, that I
would put Love in the middle, Peace and Joy on each side, and
then a high and broad banner to stretch across the tent, and
on it the word Righteousness. It is a great word, and de-
scribes more than anything else what God is, and what God
would have us to be. ' The righteous Lord loveth righteousness.' Take all that goes to make a strong man—take truth-
fulness to begin with, take purity, take patience, take love,
take energy, take gentleness. Put them all together, and if
you want to sum them up in one word it is *righteousness.*
God is ready to forgive our unrighteousness and take away
our guilt, but it is ' that the righteousness of the law may be
fulfilled in us.' God wants His children to be good as we do
ours. And what is the way ? If you believe Christ made
Himself one with you, then believe that His death is your
death, His resurrection your resurrection, His life your life.

" Sin is there, ' the law of sin in the members,' but though
sin is in the flesh, you are not in the flesh but in the Spirit,
for you live ' not under law but under grace.' As Mr. Webb
Peploe said—' If a man in the hospital were to say, you can
bury me, I am entirely dead, I *feel* it, the doctors would say
he is better.' *Feeling* dead—there is no sense in it at all.
You must *reckon* yourself dead in the person of Christ, because
Christ has gone through death, and you have gone through it
with Him. This Rom vi. 11 was one of the chief means used
to show one the truth on these subjects. As I remember
saying at the time, there were some sins which I could not

say I hated, I rather loved them, that was the mischief of
it.   One of my friends replied, 'Have you not read that you
are to reckon yourself to be dead unto sin?' Well, I saw
that it was a duty to say to sin, 'I am dead to you. You may
be lively enough, but I am dead to you. I have nothing to do
with you, whether you like it or do not like it.' And this works.
It is practicable—the old man buried as far and as long as I
remain in the faith (and why should I not remain in it?),
the new man risen, created in Christ Jesus unto righteousness
and true holiness. And the new man is the true man. We
are met here to be put right, put into harmony with God
whether for the first time or the twentieth. Nay, we have to
do it every day of our lives : to come to Christ, to hang upon
Christ, to reckon ourselves—and it is not always easy—dead
unto sin, and to rejoice in the resurrection life of Christ, to
do the will of the righteous Lord, who loveth righteousness."

The year 1892 Mr. Moody came, not as a speaker but as an
interested listener. On the Sunday he gave an evangelistic
address, and then the Bishop of Liverpool, Dr. Ryle, was beside
him as a worshipper.

Dr. Pentecost was among the speakers of that year, but we
find no record of his address. The Rev. Charles Inwood,
whose voice was to be heard again and again,—and long may
it be heard!—spoke that year, taking the somewhat strange
subject of the graven image made by Micah (Judges xvii. 3).
" We give something we possess," he said, " and call that consecration. It is perfectly right to place all that we have in
God's hand ; that is one aspect of consecration. But if you
imagine that any gift of yours can be accepted by God as a
substitute for, or equivalent to, your personal consecration,
then you are making a grave mistake. In Corinthians you
have God's idea of consecration—' They first gave their own
selves to the Lord.' Man-made wealth, man-made idols, and
man-made priests, may all go together. The religious idol
may be the most perilous of all idols. We give what we possess
to God, something that will minister to our vanity or self-
importance, something that we can worship in secret, and of
which we can be proud without losing caste among Christian
people. We consecrate ourselves to God, and then fret and
chafe at a bit of Christian work which gives no opportunity of

showing ourselves off, and bowing down before that darling secret religious idol."

It is noticed as characteristic of 1892, (surely it was of some subsequent years also), that there were prayer meetings in the Drill Hall from 9-30 to 11-30 p.m. which proved in many respects most remarkable in their quiet spiritual power. " They were not in the programme, but were the overflowings of a cup the Lord had filled. Dr. Cumming, Mr. Gregson, Mr. Grubb, Mr. Webster and others spoke as the Lord gave them utterance. The prayers were marked alike by faith and fervour. Strong men were bowed down, broken, and lifted up under the spell of an invisible but manifestly present Spirit moving upon the heart. Many rose to bear testimony. " Truly God is doing great things," so wrote Mr. Houghton in the preface of the 1892 Keswick Week.

For the next year, we dare not refer to more than two speakers and two addresses. The first speaker was Hudson Taylor, saint and missionary, his subject " The glorious Coming," his text " That blessed hope," (Titus ii. 13). " Christ's return," he testified, " is a most practical subject. In my early Christian life a friend gave me a string of passages without note or comment. It took me weeks to consider them in their context. The result was, the conviction that the hope of His Coming is a paramount New Testament motive to earnest holy service and to encouragement under trial and persecution. Someone spoke of it as cutting the nerve of missionary effort. I wish to bear testimony that it has been the greatest spur to me in missionary service. The fact that we are not to expect the conversion, we are to seek the *evangelization*—of the world in this dispensation, has prevented a discouragement that would else have led to my giving up missionary work."

The other speaker was the Rev. C. G. Moore, who by voice and pen has done amazing service to the Movement. If we could tell what some of his probing words have been to us and could get him to believe it, storm clouds that darkly gather would surely be irradiated with light. His subject that day in 1893 was " Grace for Grace." He took us to an orchard where grafting was going on, the little graft held in contact with the tree by clay which covers the point of junction. The design is to establish a fellowship which shall result in that little graft becoming a fruitful branch of that tree. "A like process we trust has been going on with many here. How disappointing to the gardener to find that, after all he has done to supply favourable conditions, the graft has not laid hold of the life of the tree ! If there be any here who have not yet entered perfect fellowship with Jesus, let me implore them by full surrender and simple trust, to do so at once. But if we enjoy this fellowship, what will be its workings in the service, difficulties, trials before us ? St. John tells us when he says of Christ ' and of His fulness have all we received and grace for grace.' John i. 16—grace taking the place of grace, a larger measure of grace supplanting a lower, because the latter, rightly used, had prepared the way for the former." "Our fellowship with Jesus is intended to make us strong, and to secure that we come out of our testings with all the wealth God designs to confer in them. Let us return to our homes to triumph in God."

The only new name we find in the list of speakers in 1894 is that of Preb. Burroughs. He spoke on " Restful Service." " There is a lot of work in the world that goes by the name of Christian work which the test of God's Word shows to be not so. We want a single eye to His glory. Anything more ? Yes. Am I doing it as Christ would do it ? And the way the Lord wants us to do our work is to have rest in it. People come from Dublin, London, Manchester to Keswick to get rest, the mountains are so restful, the lake so quiet, there is none of the throb of the busy world here, but there is here the presence of God, a God of rest and peace.

They say that in California there is a lake so high up on a mountain that it is never ruffled, the storms are down below. That is why Jesus Christ's life was so calm. Much of it seemed failure, but it was no failure, and He knew it. Therefore He was calm and restful about it, and when Pentecost came, three thousand souls were gathered in."

We dare not dilate on other features of this Convention. A second Tent, holding a thousand persons, was for the first time provided, and was generally filled. There was also a Camp with a hundred and fifty students from Universities, both these additions evincing growth of interest, and opportunity.

CHAPTER XIII

SOME STRIKING TESTIMONIES

" The long, hushed crowd has passed from Keswick's Tent,
    And I crept forth to solitude,
  To muse and ponder much in deep content,
    Mid lonely fell and wood.

" Deep into Barrow's glen I took my way;
    The trees shed down their greenest shade;
  The lofty cascade in the dying day
    Its softest music made!

" Thus let me live in joy and even in tears;
    My life, like this, a ceaseless song;
  A Day of Heaven lent from the Eternal Years;
    Nor missed in yon bright throng! "

J. ELDER CUMMING.

AMONG many leaders in the spiritual life who joined the
Keswick group in the latter half of the eighties, was
Dr. Handley Moule—already referred to—a true " father in
God " whether as Head of a College, or Bishop of a Diocese.
He spoke in 1886 on " Christian Total Abstinence "—abstinence from every evil thing. " Is there no such thing," he
said, " as a relish sometimes felt when someone we have dis-
agreed with in Christian doctrine is caught a little tripping in
Christian practice, not because there is a vindication of the
need of watchfulness, but because here is that dear and precious thing ' my opinion,' vindicated to myself? Is there no
such thing again as a jealousy for our own work, cause, reputation, which does not make it always altogether pleasant to
hear of the marked success granted to some one of another
Christian organization, or of another school of opinion, or,
perhaps, to some one not divided from us by any such lines,
but by that great demarcation that it is not ' number one? '
Is there no such thing as that? "

In 1893 a more personal note was struck. " Some years ago," said the voice we reverence so deeply, " I should not have been asked to go to Keswick, and if I had been, I should certainly not have gone. But I was staying as one of a house-party, where I found, after my arrival, there were to be consecration meetings." He described how much he wished himself away. This could not be, without breaking the courtesies of life. Words from Haggai were God's message to him, and during the after meeting, he said, " I felt it most difficult to stand, but, in the way God had spoken to me, it was more difficult *not* to stand. The calm and peace of God filled me, and I returned home at His absolute disposal. What of the nine years since ? They have been on an absolutely different plane, both as to Christian work, and as to the presence of Christ. There has indeed been failure on my part ; but every failure can now be seen to be one's own fault, and that which need not have been."

Another speaker on the same occasion was one for whose early death both England and Scotland wept—the Rev. George Macgregor. His addresses, so Scriptural and so incisive, caught the ear of the Convention as very few have done. He " stated that he heard of Keswick as a place where sanctification was treated of, and he came as a matter of purely intellectual interest ; but he had not been in the place many minutes before he found that the treatment was practical and new. Then he felt very angry, as a Scotchman, at being told anything new in theology by Englishmen ! Monday was a terribly cold night, and Tuesday a burning day. Dr. Moule brought him to the crisis, and the conflict was narrowed down at last to one point. When that very point was touched that night by Mr. Hopkins, he felt so stung that he could have sprung to his feet and left. But God led him to do a very different thing—to commit himself wholly into the Lord's hands. Mr. Meyer laid hold of him as he spoke of getting out of the boat of self, and Mr. Hopkins followed with the opportunity ' Will you get out ? ' It was to him indeed like leaping out of a boat upon the waters. ' How has it been since ? ' In temper and worry—my weak places—I have found deliverance ; not that the capacity for either has gone, but Christ has His hands on me now."

One of those to whom Mr. Macgregor bore testimony as a great helper in Christ, the Rev. F. B. Meyer, by his words spoken and written has carried the teaching of sanctification, now to crowds in the heart of London, now to gatherings at Northfield or Atalanta, and now to lonely and weary workers in India and China. His touch is so human, and withal the truth he handles so divine, that few can resist his spell. People that would not look at Keswick, would listen to *him*. The masterly way in which, side by side with the Bishop of London, he has handled social questions, has won the commendation of Christians of all Churches.

Speaking in the Tent in 1888 on GOD'S SILENCE he said, " God has not spoken to you for many a day in any fresh and vivid sense, because in your life there is something that should have been confessed, judged, and put away ; or because you have been content to think of Christ as One Who, at the time of death, shall lead you into the Father's presence forgiven. You must rise to the conviction that He has power to keep from sin and to dwell in the soul and order it. Step out and say, ' *Lord*,' and you will find that when you act on what you know to be true, the blessed hour will come when as a cloud is dispelled by the sun, so through the Spirit there shall be a new revelation of Christ's love to you. Put your *will* on Christ's side and leave Him to effect in you what you cannot effect in yourself."

A friend of a very different type, the record of whose course has well been called " Life Radiant," the Rev. F. Paynter, Rector of Stoke next Guildford, was another whose presence was an inspiration to many in those days. It was our joy earlier still to meet him at Prayer Meetings in Brighton, and later still to prove his brotherly love in acts of ministerial fellowship such as are all too rare. The life of our friend was more beautiful than his beautiful home, and the tokens of his abiding peace in God were as evident amid rain and hail in Palestine, as in the Tents of Keswick. To have known him makes one thankful to have lived !

Side by side with Mr. Paynter, it seems natural to refer to a younger man, and more robust, whose face also is always a sunbeam, and his voice a joy bell, the Rev. S. A. Selwyn, now Vicar of Sherbourne.

The same words might be used of another friend, so buoyant that he seems to have the secret of eternal youth. Who that has heard the Rev. J. J. Luce speak, who that has heard him sing, who that has known him at home, or travelled with him abroad, but has felt the old lines truer than ever,

> " 'Tis religion that can give
> Sweetest pleasures while we live " ?

Mr. Selwyn, speaking in 1894, said, " Alas that among Christians there should be any lack of tenderness. Those are the Christians whom God has to crush, perhaps at Conventions, more likely by some awful sorrow. He puts His hand upon them, not to cause them to despair, but to break into them that His love may break out of them. The Lord turned the captivity of Job, are we willing to be turned on the Lord's terms ? There is no singing in captivity, the harps are all hung up. Or if a little singing, it is in the minor key. There are minor key Christians. Let go that chain, or it may be that little spider's web of bondage which keeps you from singing the song. The Lord wants us to sing, so that men may be attracted to Him."

Speaking in 1895, Mr. Luce said, " I have been praying God to put a word in my mouth to help some younger Christians who are longing—not as a theory, sentiment, or fad—to be living in Canaan. Canaan is one of those words translated *humility*, so to live there is to live in a land in which we are nothing and Christ is all. I have a book wherein I wrote on one side the difficulties of anxious souls I had met, on the other the answers I gave to them. And the remarkable thing is, that every difficulty begins with I. *I* have so little faith. *I* feel so wicked. *I* do not feel wicked enough. And every answer to the difficulties begins with Jesus. *Jesus* said. *Jesus* shed His blood. *Jesus* is mighty to save. Until the Lord Jesus is magnified in our esteem, our difficulties will be unmet. Then He wants to lead us over Jordan. We saw Him crucified for us, but we need to see that we are crucified with Him. We saw Him risen for us, He wants to teach us what it is to be alive with His life. Dear William Reid used to say, ' It's iall n the reckoning.' And then as we do the reckoning the Spirit fulfils the promise, ' Sin shall not have dominion over you.' When He has led us over Jordan, the Lord leads us to the feast, as the Israelites kept the passover at Gilgal."

" Be doers of the word," said Mr. Luce another year, " means a great deal to some of us. I know one to whom God's will made known at such a Convention meant a sacrifice of £200 a year. Well, count the cost, and then buy of Him, for everything He sells is worth more than all He asks." Our friend's life—a life not without many a sorrow—shows that Christ is worth all the world to *him* !

One of the most striking testimonies ever given was that by the Rev. Wm. Houghton, then of Guildford. He had come from that town by the urgency of the Rev. F. Paynter, its Rector. The *British Weekly* asked him to be their correspondent. " Did you see the two articles, and note the discrepancy ? " asked Mr. Hopkins ; " the one was adverse, the other full of appreciation ; the man had got a blessing ! " And he had, and told of it by " rising in his place " and by letter, in Keswick itself, and more fully at our Brighton Dome. His ministry yielded better testimony still. It has been " a sweet savour unto God " in many places, e.g. Paris, Lausanne, Geneva (often), Clarens (at fourteen Conventions), Alexandria, Cairo and Jerusalem, to say nothing of countless addresses in the Homeland.

CHAPTER XIV

"ONE OF THE OLD PROPHETS RISEN FROM THE DEAD."

" Sweet childhood of eternal life !
Whilst troubled days and years go by,
In stillness hushed from stir and strife,
Within Thy Arms I lie."

HOW beautifully God quarries and polishes the stones for His temple. A Scotch family settled in South Africa and made it the country of their hearts and lives. The double influence was used to prepare a deep teacher for his deep work. Little did Andrew Murray, when a student in Scotland, imagine that he would come to be looked upon as the Christian patriarch of South Africa. As little did he think when preaching, in Dutch, series after series of pastoral sermons, that, translated into English, they would be read by thousands of people in the homeland. But so it was. *Abide in Christ* was an epoch-making volume ; it fell into our hands on a winter holiday among the snows. Christians everywhere were reading it, and its companion volumes were eagerly awaited. With what joy, then, did England hear that the author was coming to her shores. With what delight did thousands welcome him at Mildmay, at Keswick, and a score of other places.

It seemed to many as if " one of the old prophets had risen from the dead."

At Keswick he gave us a series of addresses, searching and inspiring to a degree. *The Keswick Week* of 1895 is very helpful, though incomplete. It quotes a few lines from the first address on " Saul's disobedience." " Samuel said to Saul, ' because thou hast rejected the word of the Lord, He hath also rejected thee,' and Saul said to Samuel, ' I have sinned.' " Was it an honest confession ? No. For he said, 'honour me, I pray thee, before the elders of my people . . that I may worship the Lord.' Is it not awful, a man convicted of witchcraft, rebellion, iniquity, content if the people think well of him, and actually going in to worship God ? Yet I fear there are souls who come to worship the Lord at Keswick who never give themselves up to obedience. I am a stranger in England, but I hear at times that Keswick is in danger, that people living worldly lives come from year to year to be edified and pleased, worshipping the Lord at Keswick, while heart and life are not given up to His service. Let us unite in a great cry to God, to uncover the terrible deception to bring us to a full realization of our place before Him."

On the Wednesday in the Pavilion, Mr. Murray spoke on two stages of Christian experience. " St. Paul's converts at Corinth were real Christians, but they had one deadly fault—they were *carnal*. And that is all the trouble in the Church with those who get a blessing and lose it again, they are *carnal*. Their state is a state of protracted infancy. You can have no more beautiful thing than an infant with its ruddy cheeks, its smiling face, the kicking of its little feet, and the movement of its little fingers. But if after six months the child were no bigger, the parents would begin to say, ' We are afraid there is something the matter ' ; and if after three years I come back and find it so, I should also find the parents sad."

" There are two marks of a babe :—it cannot help itself. Many Christians are always wanting their ministers to be nursing and feeding them. They never want to be men—never help themselves, and of course cannot help others. It is with them, as we read in Hebrews, that those who ought to be teachers need others to teach them the very rudiments of Christianity."

" The other mark of a carnal state is that sin and failure prove master. Envyings and divisions are fruits of the carnal spirit. Every sin against love is a proof that a man is living in the flesh. You say, ' I have tried to conquer it and I cannot.' That is my point, while you are carnal you cannot bear spiritual fruit ; but receive the Holy Spirit and the carnal will be conquered. It is so with love of the world, love of money, neglect of prayer. No use to write a resolution—

' I will pray more.' Let the axe strike the root of the tree.
Let the Holy Spirit cut down the carnal mind. Give over the
flesh to death ; then the Spirit of God will come in and you
will learn to love prayer, to love God and your neighbour. And
you will be possessed of humility and heavenly-mindedness."

On Thursday evening Mr. Murray spoke on the subject of
" The path of consecration," from Mark x. 37. " Grant unto
us that we may sit, one on Thy right hand, and the other on
Thy left hand, in Thy glory." " Three things these disciples
ask—Nearness to Jesus, Likeness to Jesus, Power for Jesus.
There were elements in this request which were not good, yet,
it was a large answer to Christ's enquiry, ' What would ye that
I should do for you ? ' And He is here to-night asking the
same question ; so formulate your petition and tell Jesus
what you want. Are they just these gifts—nearness, likeness,
power. Is that your heart ? "

" Note their mistakes about consecration. These men were
asking for fruit, and the root had not been planted. Like a
child sticking a branch in the sand which he calls his garden,
we are always wanting the fruit and the blessing, but Christ
wants us to have the root deep down. Again, the Father alone
could give this : how careful Christ is to honour the Father !
Some people think if we talk too much of God, Christ will lose
His place. Nay, Christ will be doubly precious. The more
I long for heaven, I find I cannot get there without Christ.
A worse mistake was that their desire had selfishness in it. It
was mixed up with carnal ideas of the kingdom. One asked
me to-day what dying with Christ means ; and another, what
being filled with the Spirit ? I have often to say, ask for
something beyond what you can understand, and let God deal
with you in the glory of His love. There is often pride in our
consecration and carnal apprehension, the desire to be happy,
holy, useful—*self* at the bottom of it. Christ does not want
His disciples to be deluded by an unsatisfactory consecration.
' Can ye drink of the cup . . . and be baptized with the
baptism . . . ? ' This is the consecration which Christ asks.
What is the cup ? What is Gethsemane (for it reappears
there) ? *The surrender of the will.* It cost Jesus a struggle to say,
' Shall I not drink of it ? ' but He conquered. So with the
baptism that He was baptized with, that was Calvary. Chris-

tians, you want the higher life, the nearness and likeness, and power of your Lord ; but He asks, 'Can you drink of my cup, and be baptized with my baptism ? ' You must die to live. Look at that splendid oak. Where was it born ? *In a grave.* The acorn was pushed under the ground, and in that grave it sprouted. For a hundred years it had stood in that grave. In that place of death it has found its life and beauty. You can get the resurrection life nowhere but in the grave of Jesus, and therein you must abide. As the oak spreads its roots under the cold, black soil farther and deeper, so the stem, branches, leaves, come upward to the sunshine. With us there is a divine beginning, glorious, sudden, when we see ourselves crucified with Christ. Let that be our daily dis-position—dead to the world, to sin, to self, to all that is not God's. Can you be baptized with this baptism unto death ? Note the answer of these men. ' We can.' Simple disciples ! They little knew what these words meant. Blessed be God, Jesus accepted the consecration. ' Ye shall drink of the Cup,' and so on. Oh, the tender Redeemer ! How did these men carry out their vow ? At the Supper they quarrelled, in the Garden they forsook Him. How, then, could Jesus accept their consecration, if it was so untrue ? At bottom it *was* true. They just meant,—'Lord, we are ready for anything.' And His loving heart said, ' I know you are.' ' '

" Can you join James and John in saying, ' We can ' ? I do not condemn you, if you rather say, trembling at all it means, at all the Cross means, ' Lord, I cannot.' Still rather say, ' Lord, in *Thy* strength I can, I will.' Then, when you get home and sign your covenant, ' Thy cup O Christ, is my cup, Thy baptism, my baptism '—Jesus will carry you through from Gethsemane to Calvary, from Calvary to Pentecost. What joy in heaven if this great company were to fall down and say, ' Yea, Lord, we can drink of Thy cup, we can be baptized even unto death.' "

The Friday was the crowning day, and Mr. Murray's surely, the crowning address. The text of it hangs on my walls, carved in the cedar of Cumberland :—" That God may be all in all " (1 Cor. xv. 28). " The whole aim of Christ's coming and of His work in our hearts is summed up in this thought— let us make it our life-motto and live it out—' That God may be all in all.' How Christ realized it in His own life. He continually spoke of Himself as sent from God. By an act of omnipotence He became the Virgin's Son, and as truly as it was the work of Almighty God thus to give His Son to live His life in the flesh, so at my conversion He gave His life into my heart.

" Christ's next step was to maintain His life in the same path. He tells us, ' I can do nothing of myself.' God is absolutely *all* and I only a vessel in which He reveals His glory.

" And notice, this was what man was created for—to be a vessel into which God could pour His wisdom and goodness, and beauty and power. So with the Seraphim, God's burning ones, His glory passes through them, they have nothing in themselves. So even with Christ. He lived among us, and day by day depended on the Father. This is the Man Who, one day in glory, will bring it about that God shall be all in all. Christ not only received His life from God and lived it in dependence on Him, but *He gave it up to God.* On the cross He carried out what had been settled in Gethsemane, and gave life back to God unto the very death. He gave up a life of humiliation, and God gave Him a life of fellowship and glory. Christian, remember that there is but one way to secure such fellowship and glory even on earth. Give your life up to God. Lose everything, and God will raise you up in glory. Christ could never have ascended to sit upon the throne, had He not begun by giving up Himself. Christ came to live out the truth, that God must be all in all.

" Is there any greater obligation on Christ to let God be all in all, than on us ? The opposite were nearer the truth. But how can we attain such a life ? Our teaching about consecration will be moonshine unless we do. Else what use of talking of giving ourselves as living sacrifices. The reason of feebleness, and failure, and lost blessing, is nothing but this—God does not get His place amongst us. *Take time and trouble to give God His rightful place.* Meditate more on your God than you have done, say, ' Thou Mighty Workman, I trust Thy power.' Then God will work wonders in you. God never works anything but wonders. It is the law of His nature.

> ' In Thy strength may I lie still,
> The clay within the Potter's hand,

Moulded by Thy gentle will,
Mightier than all command ;
Shaped and mould by Thee alone,
Now and ever more Thine own.'

" Would that I could persuade every one of you that *God
is waiting to do for you more than even you can conceive.*

" Again, sacrifice everything for God's kingdom and glory.
The root principle of Christ's life was self-sacrifice to God
for man. Every redeemed soul carries this with him unquench-
ably, but alas ! it can be smothered. The soldier says, ' everything for my King and country.' Are earthly kings to have
such devotion, and you and I merely *talk* about God being all
in all ? Nay. Let each say, ' I will sacrifice everything for
Him.' And whether in mission work away, or Christian work
or life at home, let each take as his watchword ' All to the
glory of God.'

" Now the last thought—Wait on God, for it is only God
Who can reveal Himself. Do not be afraid if people say, ' do
you want to make Quakers of us ? ' Every portion of Christ's
Body teaches something. None of you will suffer if you learn
the lesson in your closet of keeping silence before God, just
with one prayer, ' Lord, reveal Thyself in my heart.' So in
your prayer meetings. Take time to say, ' Father, let it please
Thee to come and meet with me.' You cannot find God without waiting upon Him. . These are the steps by which God may
become all in all in our lives, and by which we may be prepared
to take our part in that glorious company who shall be present
when Christ shall give up the kingdom to His Father ' that
God may be all in all.' "

We are indebted to *The Christian* for supplying us with a
full record both of an address at the minister's meeting, and
of another at the testimony meeting. Dr. Andrew Murray
spoke (on the Thursday) to ministers from Job xlii. 5, 6. " These
verses," he said, " are the passage from the first to the second
part of Job's life. You know the wonderful difference when
he had passed through this gate into the blessed life—a life of
full power as an intercessor, a life in full blessing of his soul
from God.

" There are two styles of religious life, the one that of *hearing,* the other that of SEEING. It is easier to hear, but un-

speakably better to see.   Israel was afraid of the sight of God.
How different Moses.   He saw God and only longed for fuller
vision—' Show me Thy glory.'   It is right that I should use
my mind.   I think, I read, I meditate, I then try to get hold
of the truth.   I get hold of it, and it affects my heart and
feeling.   But still there is a worm at the root of my life, some-
how the effect of teaching does not last.   Why?   Because
there has been no personal vision, no personal contact with
God.   What a minister needs is to be a man of God, as the
Old Testament prophets were called.   His mark is that he
comes from God, he is full of God, serves God and God is with
him.   If we get that. all else comes in its right place.   The
man of God has the Almighty One working in him.   But no
one can be a man of God unless he can say with Elijah, ' The
Lord God of Israel before Whom I stand.'

" We must see God.   Do not ask me how ?   When the Holy
Ghost came, the word of Jesus came true, ' Henceforth ye do
know Him and have seen Him.'   Not till we get to this point
does the vision of God fill our eyes and our heart.   Then the
unsearchable mystery of the Great Being in Heaven attracts
us, and the cry of the heart is, God take to-day the place in
my life which as God Thou art able to take.   Then, as the axe
in the hand of the woodsman, I can be used by my God.

" Let the WORD become to you the word of God, the Living
God, Who has overwhelmed you, Who has possessed you, Who
lives around you, about you, within you.   Speak the Word in
pulpit or in private as from your God.   It may be, will be, imperfect, with fear and trembling, with stammering lips, with
shame, but speak it as the word of the everlasting God.

" It is all right to *study the word*, study it twice as much as
you do.   But still more STUDY GOD, wait upon God, ask God
by the Holy Ghost to reveal Himself ; not in a fashion that
you could necessarily give an account of, but as the sun reveals
himself even through clouds.

" The root of the curse in your life is self-effort, self-strength,
self-righteousness.   You may preach loudest of any man in
England against self-righteousness, but it is in you as in Job,
till you see God and abhor yourself in dust and ashes.   What
is all this talk of crucifixion and death ?   It is like Job's feeling,
' I am undone, there is nothing left of me, I have seen God.'
That is our need.   I

"You may go away from Keswick with note-books filled with beautiful thoughts, and hearts filled with beautiful impressions. But if it be a religion of hearing it will pass in two months. 'Now mine eye seeth Thee, therefore I abhor myself and repent.' Be that your and my Keswick blessing! How shall we get it? First, has God taken the place in our heart and life He desires and deserves? When I think of the everlasting God waiting to enter and kept by me outside, then I abhor myself. Let us set our heart on God, He must be all. Second, you find a God who can help. I set myself to search out the name of God or allusions to it, and I am amazed at what I have found. In the Psalms e.g. God sometimes is named in every verse. Go through the Bible thus, the discoveries will surprise and the conviction will amaze you. Leave the platform of the self life and die with Job—nay, with Jesus—to be raised with Job—nay, with Jesus, to a new life of power and blessing."

Our readers would hardly forgive us if we closed this chapter without giving the personal testimony of this revered teacher. This also we take from *The Christian*. "The first ten years of my Christian life were spent manifestly on its lower stage. There was all the time a burning dissatisfaction and restlessness. I used to sit at Bloemfontein thinking, What is the matter with me? Here am I knowing that God has justified me through the blood of Jesus, but I have no power for service. Though all thought me one of the most earnest of men, I was disappointed. A missionary said to me one day, 'Brother, when God puts a desire into the heart He means to fulfil it.' I thought of that a hundred times.

"A book you know—Mrs. Gatty's *Parables from Nature*—helped me as it told of the old cricket saying to the younger 'my child, your Creator never made any one without preparing a place for him; wait, and you will find yours in due time.' Later on the young cricket said, 'When these people came and built a house and lit a fire, when I got into the corner of the hearth near the fire, I knew that was the place God had made for me.'

"By and by (in 1860) my home was moved to Worcester, and God poured out His Spirit on us there and around, as He had done on many in Ireland the year before, and I wrote (in Dutch) *Abide in Christ*. Understand, a minister or author may be led to say more than he has experienced. I had not experienced all I then wrote, I cannot say that I have yet. But if we honestly seek to trust God, and to receive His truth He will make it live in our hearts. But I warn you, the most beautiful *thoughts* cannot help you unless you go to God Himself to give you THE REALITY.

"In 1870 and after, the accounts in *The Christian* about 'Oxford' and 'Brighton' helped me. And if I were to speak of consecration I might tell you of an evening in my study at Capetown, but I cannot call it a deliverance, for I was still struggling. Then I was exercised about the fulness of the Spirit and sought it as earnestly as I knew how. Still there was failure. God forgive it! Yet through all the stumblings, God led me without any special experience I can point to, to the possession of more and more of His blessed Spirit.

"Every day I placed myself before God as a vessel to be filled with the Spirit, and God gives me the blessed assurance that He has. If there is one lesson that I learn day by day it is that God worketh all in all.

"I think some of you fail just here. You do not believe heartily that God is working out your salvation. You believe it of a painter and his painting, of a workman and his work, but cannot believe that the everlasting God is working out the image of His Son in you. Try to alter this and to say with me, my home is always the abiding love of my Father who is in Heaven. 'Are you satisfied? Have you all you want?' God forbid! But with my whole soul I can say, I am satisfied with Jesus. Yet this is only the beginning, let us trust Him for more and more."

It seemed best in writing of this one year to let but one voice be God's mouthpiece. Not but that other voices spoke, and with all the gift and grace of other years. But they were heard often, dear Andrew Murray only this once. How many of us looked back through the strain of the South African War, and the healing days since, to this wonderful series of messages, and looked up to God, Who is as near Stellenbosch as Keswick, praying Him to continue His love to this patriarch and friend, making him,

"Right down to the golden West,
Everywhere blessing, everywhere blest."

CHAPTER XV

"YEARS OF THE RIGHT HAND OF THE MOST HIGH"

" 'Lord, Thou hast declared that sin shall not have dominion over me ; I believe that this word cannot be broken, and, therefore, helpless in myself, I rely upon Thy faithfulness to save me from the dominion of sin. [Name your besetment and sin.] Put forth Thy power, O Lord Christ, and get Thy glory in subduing my flesh.' Trust Him to make His word good, and wait the event. Sooner shall heaven and earth pass away than sin, any sin, thus left with Christ to be subdued, shall reign over thee."

ROMAINE.

THE years that followed the visit of Dr. Andrew Murray confessedly missed his strong personality. The writer of the Introduction of *The Keswick Week* for 1896 says : " Recent illness affected Mr. Fox, and kept Mrs. Bannister away ; and the chairman's many labours and winter's troubles made him at last accede to the requests of friends to take less of the burden on himself."

In 1897 the following occurs : " The pressure of the crowds did not seem so great this year, and we believe there were about four hundred fewer present."

But this was only temporary, for in 1898 " The attendance was larger than ever, proved by the railway tickets taken, as well as by the crowded Tent, even when four other meetings were going on at the same time."

In 1899 we read of thronged trains " divided several times over, the impossibility of getting rooms not bespoken, and the crowding of Tent, Pavilion and Drill Hall at one time."

In 1900 many foreign friends were present, " and a large number of clergy, missionaries, and other workers. The side meetings were full, except that for young men, which felt the war blanks."

1896 witnessed the consolidation of the evangelistic work of the Convention, Lord Overtoun, Rev. John McNeill, Mr. Lane, and Mr. W. Wilson leading that important side of the work. The foreign missionary meetings of the year also reached their high water mark.   " Canon Taylor Smith's statement as to the origin of his mission work went to every heart."

Pasteur Coillard spoke of his work on the Zambesi, and the presence of the friend from Jerusalem whose letter and donation, ten years ago, became the starting point of the Keswick missionary movement, was of deep interest. But everything else was in a measure forgotten when, on Saturday, it was announced that we met on the anniversary of the massacre of the Ku-Cheng Missionaries in China ; and when it became known that there was present, somewhere in the meeting (almost in hiding), one who was brutally attacked in the massacre, and was left for dead, but eventually spared, to bear about in her body ' the marks of the Lord Jesus.' "

But China was not only brought to our thoughts by the blessed dead, but by living saints. Hudson Taylor told of the wonderful conversion of an Agnostic. " ' You, a gentleman, and one of the literati,' said the Mayor, ' preaching the doctrine of the foreigners ! I wonder you are not ashamed.' ' I simply preach because I cannot keep it in ; it has made me so glad,' he said. That is what we want here, men so filled with the Spirit of God and with His truth that they will overflow, because they cannot help it. That Chinese convert preached Christ as able to take away power of opium, gambling, and every other vice. A bad man looking into his face said, ' You know me, and know my life ; can your Saviour save me ? ' ' He can.' ' When, and how ' ? ' At once, and for ever.' The man walked to his home, a gambling hell, turned out bad women and men, and said, ' This house will be closed and whitewashed, and then re-opened for the preaching of the gospel.' When Christ comes it is unmistakable. The man's family was converted ; faith in the same Lord and in the same Word will have the same effect here.

" You are not merely to get life out of Christ. When He says ' I am the Vine,' He includes root, stem, and branch, leaf, flower, and fruit. So in the body, the life permeates every part. It requires the whole life of Christ, not a gift from Christ, to keep (spiritually) even a finger alive. What we have to do is to abide ; the branch abides in the vine, as the babe on its mother's breast, and everything is done for it."

Next morning at the early prayer meeting the address was from the lips of the Rev. J. J. Luce. (Luke iv. 32.) " A lovely picture of Christian unity. How may we help to carry on and carry out this work ? By one heart and mind with Jesus. If you want to help the unity of the Spirit, mind that you live in unity with Christ and be filled with the Holy Ghost. This there must be if we are to have not a sham, not a formula, but a real manifestation of the oneness of the Body of Christ. When we get back to our homes let us more earnestly desire to attend the prayer meeting. Do not mind whether people drop their h's. Remember the Lord knows the heart, and learn to bear and forbear. . . . Speak well of other denominations. I am a debtor to the whole Church. I have learnt from ' Brethren ' much concerning preparation for Christ's return. I am a debtor to the Society of Friends. I had judged them in ignorance ; I never knew how they looked at the Sacraments. I have found it helpful to observe from their standpoint. I am a debtor to the Wesleyans—much helped by their earnest-ness, warmth and power. I am a debtor to Baptists and Con-gregationalists. How they have helped me in their prayer meetings ! I can think of no denomination from which I have not received help. So let us try in practical life, and in our disposition to Christians who think differently and are not in the same outward church, to help one another at home and away."

From the Report of 1897 we can quote only what is said of three memorable testimonies. The Rev. F. Paynter told how God, meeting with him, had changed him from a " stiff " churchman into one loving all the brethren in Christ Jesus. The testimony is more fully given in a sermon in *Life Radiant*. " Two young converts called on me, and quoting ' Be filled with the Spirit,' remarked that it was a command. Their statement chimed in with the blessing in Glasgow on people of all ages and occupations described by the Rev. H. B. Macart-ney. All this drove me to my knees seeking as the great object of my desire that God would glorify Himself in me by filling me with His Spirit. After prayer the blessing came, and so pervades me that I now seem hardly able to speak or think of anything else. I can only praise for such boundless grace to so unworthy and sinful a creature as I know myself to be. I

ask your prayers that the axe may be laid at the root of all
spiritual pride, for after such a season of enlargement, unless
the Lord withhold him, Satan is sure to assail me in a fearful
manner ; so I rejoice with trembling."

The Rev. J. Roscoe of Uganda, testified that the searching
and convicting power of God had shown them that the lack of
the fulness of the Spirit in their lives told on the heathen, and
on converts too. So they separated themselves for days, to
seek what God meant by the command " Be filled with the
Spirit." He met the need as at Pentecost. Quickening of
converts, and ingathering from among the heathen began.
" As the Nile with its annual inundation, and the Ruwenzori
with its eternal snow at the very equator, is witness of outward
power," so this missionary history revealed boundless possibilities in grace.

The closing witness was Dr. Pierson. It almost seemed as
if he had been sent from America to take the place of Dr.
Andrew Murray, now back in Africa, with this happy difference
that Dr. Pierson was to be with us again and again. He told
of the cost and humiliation it was to him to witness, how that
when work was vigorous and consecration unreserved, disposition and character remained untransformed. Again, he told
how God had searched him there, and when Mr. Peploe and
Dr. Andrew Murray visited America in 1895 and spoke of the
power of God as to character, inviting any to stand who felt
a need of claiming that power, he was one to stand. Then he
found that this step was the last one of the old way of failure,
and now he could bring others, even at home, to prove the
change. He felt he owed so much to those sent from Keswick
that he " must see the plant in its native soil," so, though it
involved four months delay, with a daughter home from Japan
after nine years work, he and his wife had waited on in
England for Keswick, and, as they were starting next morning
they asked prayer for keeping, and for blessing on similar work
in America. " A throb of response answered this plea, and
after being led in audible prayer, we scattered with a sense of
God upon us."

In 1898 two features are emphasized. " The prominence
given to the after meeting was a large secret of blessing. No
undue stress was laid on any visible act of surrender, but there

was a wholesome insistence on present and open committal."
The other was that the Saturday morning gathering was for
praise only. One behind the scenes said there were three or
four times as many petitions for praise as ever before. Then
came texts as usual from the speakers, Dr. Moule gave Philippians i. 1,—the two spheres of the Christian " The church
which is in Christ," " The church which is in Philippi." The
Rev. C. A. Fox gave, " If we suffer we shall also reign with
Him." and (to pass over many), the Rev. C. Inwood gave
Numbers vi. 24-26, so that the final word was " renewed
blessing." The same chronicler says, " The desire for definite
conversions expressed earnestly at the commencement was
answered, and evangelistic effort was very active, *hardly a
court in Keswick being left unvisited !* " and then goes on to
describe the contrasts of the people who came themselves
seeking blessing, " contrasts of age and strength, from young
men, in their strong and vigorous health and equally vigorous
purpose to be all for God, to the veteran workers whose long
lives of service endorse all He is of grace and goodness. Contrasts of spheres of service," from icy snows to tropical heat.
Contrasts in very appearance ; a household of Oxford or Cambridge undergraduates, and a household of Manchester mill
workers. All seemed equally eager to drink of the brook by
the way and so lift up the head.

1899 was the SILVER WEDDING of the Convention. Greater
numbers poured in, and Tent, Pavilion, and Drill Hall were
all filled. Of new speakers we note Bishop Peel, of Mombasa.
He told of what Keswick teaching meant in the mission field :
" Oh, the *joy* in a heathen city, to know that it is *God* that
works." Ten years before, a study of sanctification had led
him to leave all with Him, and " Oh, the *rest* to know that
Jesus was to do all, that, as He never worked without His Father,
so *we* were never to work without Him. The one thing for us
to do is to stand by His side for Him to use. Blessed life !
Not only sin blotted out, but sin overcome, and the fears and
stains of the future blotted out, because there was only Jesus
seen in it." Preaching on union with Christ, he showed how
this was possible not only to loving trust like that of Mary
Magdalene, but of backsliders like Peter, and doubters like
Thomas, for the risen Christ vouchsafed fellowship to all three.

The Church of Scotland sent us, as indeed before and often after, the Rev. J. R. Macpherson.

The previous year he strikingly began an address on the oath of God, by referring to the forest of hands raised the night before in testimony of the divine deliverance, and the still larger number raised in token of longing for such deliverance. " God's oath to Abraham," he said, " pledged Him to make us a grant, this namely, deliverance ' out of the hand of our enemies ' (Luke i. 74) : not help in struggling to overcome them, not assistance in a life-long contest against them, but deliverance from them. It does not mean that your enemies will all be dead ; but God's promise is deliverance from their power. ' That wicked one toucheth you not.' Willingly or unwillingly, some sin has been yielded to. God's pledge is that the dominion is broken. Nothing less than this can satisfy His words. Accept from the pierced hand of Christ deliverance from the hand of your enemies."

This year he went over the well-worn ground of Romans vi., and came back to the same point of " supreme deliverance. Saviour, I claim it, I dare to reckon myself dead even to the sin revealed to me by God . . . and, thank God, there is more than that, ' Alive unto God ' ; quickened by the resurrection power of God Himself, through or in Christ."

Nonconformity, again, sent us one of its most prominent representatives in Mr. Meyer. Jacob's second visit to Bethel was his subject, and he began, " Let me lay my hand on the cords of memory back in your life's story twenty, thirty years, to the day when, staff in hand, a lonely soul, you fled to the moorland waste, and lay down on one of the boulder stones in the sleep of utter exhaustion.

" Do you remember how God appeared to you that night, and how at the foot of the ladder you vowed to be His for evermore. You remember that vision, that altar, that vow, here in Keswick, perhaps, the little bedroom, or the spot on the hills, where, under the tremendous pressure of His hand, you vowed you would be all for God. Alas ! the light has gone from the sky, the ladder from the earth, and your vows have been unkept.

" You remember another time—perhaps here—you were again alone, you had a vision of God, indeed a tremendous wrestle, but you thought you yielded, and you began to limp as the result. Why is it that, since both Bethel and Peniel, your life has again been a failure. Has there been any insincerity in it, I ask, or have you been building your house near Shechem (the world), or winking at idolatry in your home ? In any case, ' *Arise, go up to Bethel, and dwell there.*' (Gen. xxxv. 1 ; compare John i. 51). When Christ ascended, He cast the ladder of His glory swaying between earth and heaven as the bridge of communication. We have access, yes, and we have power. Bury the old man, as Jacob buried earrings [1] and teraphim, ' and put on the new man which after God '—in the likeness of God—' is renewed in righteousness and true holiness.' Christ wrought a new creation for us at His resurrection, but by a momentary act we appropriate it now."

The United Free Church sent the Rev. W. D. Moffat, who, as Convener of the Bridge of Allan Convention, wrought a standing work. He said : " ' What is the meaning of Paraclete ? ' asked a lady. The disciples never asked this, for they had known Christ as their Paraclete for three years. The word covered every aspect of Christ's relationship to them. And we know that He did send them another Paraclete who was to those disciples all that Jesus had been, and more. One of the things most striking in Christ's promises of the Comforter is His Personality. We all believe in it, but have we received the Holy Spirit as our Companion ? Do we know His fellowship in our life ? He comes working in us, as Christ in the twelve, fitness for God's service and presence. Our Saviour took His disciples into His heart, and found His way into their hearts. He has sent the Paraclete to do the same."

Another representative of the same church present—none of us knew it would be for the last time—was dear George Macgregor. Who can forget his application of the narrative of the woman healed of Christ after she had been given up by the physicians ? " For twenty, thirty, forty years, your life has been like hers, a life of disease. Day by day your spiritual strength has been sapped by sin. You are saying it is so hard to be a Christian. You have to whip yourselves up to your religion. What disappointment, what tragedy lies in this meeting ! . . If the woman had thought of her neighbours,

---

[1] Gen. xxxv. 4.

she would have been panic-stricken. But she was thinking
of Christ, and all her energy was to get to Him. So you.
Think of Him, and of His power. It seems incredible that
here and now, the sins that have beset you for a lifetime should
be broken, but Christ is very God of very God. Think of His
power until you say, God can ; and of His love until you say,
God will. And then you may catch yourself saying, ' If I
can but touch Him I shall be whole.' Then your energy will
be taken up, not with the address or after meeting, but the
effort to get at *Him* and His healing . . . you may be suddenly
cured as she was. Do not stagger at it. Remember it is
God, and, when He begins to work, He can work rapidly. The
sin that has troubled you for twenty-five years may be broken
to-night."

> " Oh, touch the hem of His garment,
>   And thou, too, shalt be free ;
>   His saving power, this very hour,.
>   Shall give new life to thee ! "

Those who have the *Keswick Week* for 1899 should read every
word of this wonderful address, and of the one that follows—
that also alas, from a voice soon to be stilled—" The Bible in
Three Words," by the Rev. C. A. Fox. And others by Dr.
Cumming, Mr. Hopkins, and Mr. Webb-Peploe.

But we must quote a few lines from speakers not so constantly
heard. The Rev. J. H. Battersby gave a striking illustration
of the words " yet not I," " from a cathedral organ, listened
to with rapture. If it could speak it might say, it is true it was
from me these sounds proceeded, but it was he who sits at the
keys who produced them." And this—" We took our seats
in the tram, and the driver simply caused the arm on the roof
to rise till it touched the cable, and that moment the power
from the cable moved the car. The tram might say, I moved,
I carried the passengers, yet not I. By myself I am utterly
powerless, but I was filled with a power not my own."

Keswick owes much to quiet, almost unseen, helpers like the
Rev. C. Lea Wilson. He spoke of The angel of the Lord en-
camping round His people (Ps. xxxiv. 7), and walking with
His people, ay, in the fire (Dan. iii. 28). " The body is the last
thing to be yielded ; here it was a real yielding, but with that
came the angel."

In every way a remarkable address on the Second Advent by Dr. White deserves perusal : " 345 verses in the Old, 385 in the New Testament speak of the Second Coming. When God has put 730 verses in His Book about it, it is time we looked into it. The first book and the last book of the New Testament ever written—1 Thessalonians and Revelation—are filled with the subject. . . . There are five crowns and *all* connected with special service, and there is special honour for all who love His appearing. There are seven wonderful prayers in 1 and 2 Thessalonians, and in the first, Christ's Coming is an incentive to unity. If Christians were looking for it they would not be casting stones at one another.

" Is prophecy practical ? It is that He may make us ' unblameable in holiness before God our Father at the coming of Jesus Christ.' It is that we may be ' preserved blameless ' thereunto. A Christian man born again is but a Christian baby, and our churches are just full of such, and the time of ministers is taken up with nursing them."

The Rev. E. L. Hamilton spoke of thirsting for holiness, for happiness, for sympathy, for love. To each the answer is Christ's own word, " Let him come unto Me and drink."

Pastor Soltau spoke from Ezekiel xxxvi. The taking away the stony heart and saving from uncleanness, and the filling with the river that shall flow with healing and life to all nations.

At the Ladies' Meetings Miss Nugent said : " The first step is to yield your will to God, to give way to Jesus. Search out the contrast of 1 Samuel xxii. 2. If you can make a worse case for yourself than those who came to David, you must be a remarkable person. But of those very people David made some of his ' mighty men.' "

Mrs. Bannister spoke on putting forth the hand of faith and touching Jesus. " We must be *real* for this contact, and must believe He *does* heal."

Mrs. Penn-Lewis, (Hebrews vi. 17–20), " Have you learned to anchor ? God is obliged to do the shaking, because you do not anchor. He never changes. It is not what you feel but what He says."

Miss Gollock spoke on " Others," and on Galatians ii. 20, " Not I, but Christ." " You see the bailiff is put out, and the Master dwells within."

Mrs. Tottenham closed with the admirable reminder " that we are not going to live a sort of fairy life floating about in sunshine, nor, on the other hand, a life of terrible experiences. Whatever it may be, it will never be a solitary life but one united to Jesus. It will be a tested life, a separated life, a supplied life. Alas ! it must be an opposed, but it may be a victorious life. God has said that those who wait on Him shall renew their strength. Wait on Him continually, and victory shall follow."

While referring to the Ladies' meetings it is impossible not to turn to the graphic chapter in Dr. Harford's book entitled *Women at Keswick.* It is from the pen of Miss Sophia Nugent.

" When the first convention took place," she writes, " that most beloved and far-sighted servant of the Lord, Mrs. Harford-Battersby, arranged that Ladies' meetings should be held.

" They gathered in the little school-room, the number present being small," but the results were large. " One of the first-fruits was a lady of Keswick, who yielded strong will and high intellect to her Master, and was used for the blessing of many others all the rest of her life.

" The first meetings were to have been under the leading of Mrs. Pearsall Smith, but when she was unable to come, Mrs. Michael Baxter was invited to take charge. She also was hindered in coming, after having accepted, and the opening meetings came to the care of Mrs. Compton, well known then in conducting missions with great blessing.

" Another who took part was Miss Harford-Battersby, sister of the founder, whose strong faith and courage were greatly instrumental in the Convention being held that year. The second year Mrs. Baxter took charge, and did so, to the blessing of many, until 1883." In 1885 Mr. Bowker the then Chairman, committed the care of the meetings, at the suggestion of Mrs. Battersby, to Mrs. Bannister and Miss Nugent. " Year by year the gatherings increased in number, and far outgrew the Lecture Hall, which had become a sacred place of meeting with God."

During its tenure " many beloved names come to mind : Mrs. Hatt Noble, Mrs. Albert Head among those called Home ; and Miss Lilias Trotter, witnessing now among the heathen to the power of His Resurrection. In 1897, Mrs. Penn-Lewis shared in prayer, and in 1898 gave her first address there.

" When a memorable missionary meeting of 1886 was held, bringing into focus many incidental allusions to the great Commission, and a still more memorable one of 1887 followed, it was as the breath of spring and the touch of rain upon the waiting blossoms. To this call, women were the first to respond and an appeal for ten ladies for Palestine found a deep welcome, and, before long, the ten were ready. Since then the ' women which publish the tidings have become a great host ' (Ps. lxviii. 11, R.V.), and over the whole Church of God—now greatly penetrated with the call of surrender which Keswick gave—the glorious trust and the call to carry it out has been heard. Dr. Hudson Taylor gave as his reckoning that two-thirds of those of the China Inland Mission were ' among the heathen ' as the result of Keswick. It was the conviction of the missionary call heard at Keswick, following on the inspiring ministry of the Rev. C. A. Fox, which led to ' The Olives ' being opened as a sphere of preparation for missionary work, from which some two hundred have gone forth to the ' Regions beyond,' to all of whom the teaching of Keswick has been a penetrating influence.

" Thank God afresh for the teaching which sends to His feet in deep humiliation, and then in the abandonment of self and all trust in it, sends to His Throne to receive the in-dwelling which is the only power to live His love before others.

" A young girl, helpless to move, wrote in answer to a friend, ' This Convention has made me able to say—I never could before—" We thank Thee for our creation." ' With feeble hands she wrote the account for others of the first Tent missionary meeting before she was called Home.

" Away among the heathen is one, the centre of a large household, being prepared as a crown for her Lord—trained to be His witness. Her inspiration to go forth was what Keswick brought to her of the boundless love which sacrificed, rose, and ascended to give the Holy Spirit to indwell and empower, to serve and to win, those most out of reach."

We pass to speak of THE KESWICK MISSIONARY MEETING for the closing year of the century.

Mr. Robert Wilson, after giving out a hymn, deputed the duties of the chair to General Hatt Noble. Mr. Head read greetings from Mr. Inwood. Dr. Cumming went into the body of the meeting and received hundreds of precious papers with gifts or promises. Mr. Meyer detailed a visit to India, a walk through the great Indian temples, one of which cost £4,000,000, but close beside it scenes that would not be tolerated in Europe. He breakfasted one day with C.M.S. men and supped with S.P.G. missionaries. He also saw Miss Amy Wilson-Carmichael, and their thoughts winged themselves from India to the home of the dear father of them all in Cumberland. Starting next day to Northfield to visit Mr. Moody and then going to Blankenburg, Mr. Meyer asked for prayer.

Before calling on three out of the five of the Mission's daughters who were present, to address the meeting, the chairman asked for a few words from Mr. Wilson. Though much weakened by illness he spoke of his dear adopted daughter, and conveyed her love to those at Keswick, adding, " She has the work of the evangelization of the heathen very much at heart, and whilst there were circumstances which might have called her home, she felt that for Jesus' sake her place was there with Mr. and Mrs. Walker, unless some call should come from God Himself to make it otherwise."

The Saturday Missionary Meeting, always a season of great interest and blessing, was begun by a benediction from Mr. Wilson. Then followed the rising of some hundred and fifty missionary brothers and sisters, at the call of Mr. Eugene Stock. The Rev. John Wilkinson prayed for them and for future missionaries. Then came addresses from many of those present : first the Rev. George Hunter from China, " with a zeal that seemed apostolic." He spoke of a journey on which he had baptized 192 believers, whilst they had twenty-two places of worship, thirteen of them provided by the converts.

Dr. Anderson, from Safed in Galilee, spoke of the conversion of a persecuting Jew.

Rev. J. Marriott, from Samoa, recalled the advance since John Williams, soon to be a martyr, went there in 1830.

Mr. James Johnson, with skin of ebony, and words full of force and full of grace, pleaded for Africa.

Miss Harding, from Bengal, spoke of their isolation, two Zenana workers, twenty-five miles from any English person or any Christian. A Hindoo said to her : " Government sends out rulers, armies, educationalists ; our intellects are reached, but it is the missionaries who touch the hearts. You English ladies have the key of India in your hands. You win our homes. I wonder you do not do it more quickly."

Miss Craven spoke of Madagascar, Miss Howard of Japan, Miss Gabb of South Africa.

Bishop Tugwell quoted the words of Lord Cranbourne, " I call on this meeting to pledge itself to the Christianity of the British Empire."

Archdeacon Fair, after thirty years' work among the Indians, and Dr. Arthur Lancaster, fresh from the Afghan Frontier, spoke of those spheres ; and then Miss Nicholson of work among the Moslems in Palestine.

There had been intervals of hymns and prayers by Mr. Webb-Peploe and another. After an address by Pastor Soltau, the offertory was received, after the singing of

" When I survey the wondrous Cross,"

and the words,—

" I will be, Lord, I will be, whate'er Thou dost want me to be ;
I will do, Lord, I will do, whate'er Thou dost want me to do ;
I will go, Lord, I will go, where'er Thou dost want me to go."

CHAPTER XVI

THE NEW CENTURY

" Here from Heaven
Relit in secret, prophet souls descend,
To kindle the quenched altars of the world ;
Bearing aloft in folded hands of prayer,
Safe through this windy world the Fire Divine."
C. A. Fox.

THE new century opened sadly. Our special messenger of love and trust, the Rev. C. A. Fox, was laid low for many months, and then was carried to " the mountains of myrrh and the hills of frankincense." His last little book, *Green Pastures and Golden Gates*, was dedicated " In thankful memory of five and twenty years' unbroken fellowship with beloved brethren at Keswick Convention, and of innumerable personal mercies connected therewith ; and in deep gratitude to Almighty God for the unspeakable joy of seeing countless lives, drawn from far and near, transfigured by Divine truth under the shadow of Skiddaw, and now dispersed through the world as His glad witnesses." So this " Great Heart " went in to see the King !

To add sorrow to sorrow, in the full vigour of early manhood, with scarcely a premonition, came the summons to George Macgregor, " Come up higher " ; and he went, to such service as the King of the worlds has for His soldiers, in other spheres. To his comrades in arms, and to hundreds who hung upon his words, his loss seemed, and seems, irreparable, for he was cast in a mould not easy to be found amongst us. When his biography came out, it was manifest that he had absorbed the later learning, and was more ready than the rest of us to accept some of the conclusions of criticism. *We* needed the lesson, lest we should refuse the " more light and truth " which

" breaks forth from God's Word." Perhaps others needed it still more, to inspire them with confidence in the Keswick circle as being broad-minded as well as large-hearted. Macgregor's place, and it was a very high place, upon our platform, surely showed that while contending earnestly for the faith once delivered unto the Saints, its leaders can welcome men of many minds and can include in their number, so long as there is the true ring of spiritual life, those who keep well abreast of the times. As the Introduction of *Keswick Week* of 1900 says : " Keswick is not a place for Bible Readings only, or chiefly, but a pool of Bethesda, where spiritual wholeness is to be sought and found ; where the Lord's question is, ' What wilt thou that I should do unto thee ? ' Not ' What wouldest thou like to do with My grace ? ' "

It was poor compensation for such losses that a new tent was presented to the trustees. We read of it under that name in the 1901 record. In subsequent years it was known as " the Skiddaw Tent," while the old tent was called " the Eskin "—each from the street in which each stood.

It is a happy sight to see the white canvas unfurled year by year, and stretched from the poles with their familiar flags. It is a mournful sight to see canvas furled, poles lowered, and platforms and floors broken up. Like Peter, we would have the tabernacles always standing on the transfiguration ground ; but like Peter, we have to be reminded that they are but for a little. A life in which their lessons are lived out, that is " the true tabernacle which the Lord hath pitched and not man."

With the new century came a new Vicar at St. John's, the Rev. Henry Venn Elliott, who gave place, however, in 1904 to the Rev. H. Gresford Jones. Preaching the opening sermon that year, Mr. Jones spoke of it as a unique privilege to welcome those who had come thus to seek God, and he prayed that " through these gatherings, under the guidance and power of the Holy Spirit, there may be unprecedented gain to the whole Church of Jesus Christ."

Though Mr. Jones had to decline a missionary Bishopric offered to him, he was not allowed to remain long at Keswick, but was promoted to a more stirring and influential post, his place at St. John's being filled by the Rev. Morley Headlam, who has shown a hearty appreciation of the work of the Convention. At the mother church, Crosthwaite, where is Southey's tomb, Canon Rawnsley has for long years exercised a unique ministry. It was our joy years ago to hear an earnest gospel sermon, preached to the crowded congregation there, by the Rev. F. Baldey, of Southsea, and prebendaries and other clergy who have come up for the Convention are to be heard there on these occasions. In the Congregational Church the value of the annual gatherings has always been recognized, and never more than under the present pastor, the Rev. W. T. Herd. For some years Mr. Meyer was there on one of the Sundays for a special Communion service. Recently Dr. Harry Guinness has often been the preacher, while Mrs. Penn Lewis has there found a welcome for her burning and impressive ministry. Wesleyans and other Methodists have thrown open their places not only to ministers of their own number, like the Rev. John Brash, but to others, like Mr. Hudson Taylor, or the Rev. George Grubb. One year Mr. Grubb's voice was heard on the Sunday in Victoria Hall. One recent year in the place where " Brethren " meet to " break bread," Mr. Daniel Crawford was one of the speakers. The Friends have their meeting, too, and in fact the Sundays at Keswick at Convention time would tax many reporters; the largest gathering of all being the overflow service in the Tent in which bishop, presbyter, or layman may be heard proclaiming the unsearchable riches of Christ.

Going back to the weekdays, the newest name on the list of speakers in 1901 was that of the Rev. James Mursell. We can quote but two sentences : " On Bishop Patteson's body, after he was martyred, were found five wounds, beautiful symbols of a life utterly devoted to Jesus Christ." . . . " ' Well-pleasing to God ' does not mean well-pleasing to self. If I begin to please myself, (soon) I abhor myself in dust and ashes. But if I will but live the life that has Him only for its King, and Keeper, and Lord, then through His mercy, even while dwelling here on earth, I shall have this testimony, that I please God."

One dare not keep on quoting more familiar speakers, but room must be found for these sentences by the Rev. George Wilson, of Edinburgh : " I fought this truth, till I was driven from my trenches with a crushed and broken heart. I stood up for the defence of the self-life in the name of a half-blind philosophy, and, it was only when I saw that a Christian conqueror is a conquered man, that I recognized that the place of the self-life was the place of the denied and the place of the crucified. . . . St. Paul had a vision. He was obedient to the heavenly vision, in which he saw the appalling condition of a lost world. He took up and carried to the last the burden, not of theological problems, but of perishing souls."

In 1902 the Convention, like all gatherings in England, felt the momentousness of the call of God to our nation in the illness of King Edward, compelling the postponement of the Coronation. So with a feeling of deep solemnity the thousands met. Keswick was felt to be a place in which to discover one's sin. " REALITY stamps every utterance," wrote a minister present for the first time ; " one feels it everywhere—in prayer and song, in private talk and public speech, and in look and manner. The intellectual level of the addresses has been astonishingly high—I have never seen it equalled ; and yet I have never detected one word that was self-conscious or egotistical, or that savoured of intellectual display. There has been no clever talk *about* holy things, but a lowly, self-forgetting showing forth of the things themselves."

The two tents were full to overflowing. Two great mission preachers, Canon Aitken and John McNeill, spoke with their old power. On Monday evening Captain Tottenham announced as the opening hymn—

> " Stand still and see, yea, see to-day,
> New wonders of redeeming grace."

In the other tent Mr. Head gave as the key-note Isaiah xliii. 19, " Behold I will do a new thing." A telegram of tender sympathy and love was sent to dear Mr. Robert Wilson. Dr. Pierson and Dr. Moule, the latter just nominated as Bishop of Durham, took as their Bible Readings, one—The Witness of Scripture to Christ, and the other—The Witness of Christ to Scripture. A few words must be quoted from Canon Aitken's address on Thirsty Christians. " Wherever I go I find any number of them. We cannot be satisfied with yesterday's blessing. But I am thinking of a different thirst. When we look back on the days of our first love and say, It is not with me now as it was then, my zeal is flagging, I am beaten by almost every foe ; are we to remain in unsatisfied thirst ? Nay. ' Come ye to the waters.' You have heard it said, I will go to Keswick. If the soul had said, I will go to Jesus, it would have been a shorter cut every way. Yet there is something hopeful in this thought of receiving blessing where others have been blessed. When Jesus cried saying, ' If any man thirst, let him come unto Me and drink,' He showed a heart of sympathy for the thirsty ones. He says *any* man. There is room in that word for the backslider. If you are saying I have not been thoroughly true to God, I feel even *far* from Him to-night, you are one of the *any* men. Or is your trouble, ' My lips are sealed ? ' you are going to find them unsealed, ' Out of you shall flow rivers of living water.' ' He that cometh to Me shall never hunger ; he that believeth on Me shall never thirst.' Say, ' Lord, I am sick and tired of myself, but I do what Thou tellest me, *I come*, I get a little nearer to Thy pierced feet,' and you will find that ' He satisfieth the longing soul.' "

It was about this time that a young clergyman first took part in the Convention at Keswick, who was to be one of the strongest forces there. John Stuart Holden had been in earlier days an evangelist of power and note. His debt to Cambridge he has repaid by starting a Camp for Cambridge men at Keswick. His gifts as an evangelist have developed into remarkable pastoral gifts at St. Paul's, Portman Square, and his voice, though one of the weakest, is listened to with intensity of interest on each side of the Atlantic. Speaking in 1903 on " God's Desire and God's Dynamic," he began with a story of Mr. Moody interrupted by a child's cry. " ' What's the matter ? ' he asked. ' She's lost,' was the reply. ' Bring her to me,' said Moody. And holding her up in his arms he asked, ' Does this child belong to any one here ? ' ' Yes, she's mine,' shouted a man. ' Well, come and fetch her.' And putting the child into her father's arms, he said, ' That is what Jesus Christ died to do—to take up lost bairns and put them into their Father's arms.' Now for what purpose," asked Mr. Holden, " have I been put back by Jesus Christ into my Father's arms ? That I may be made like unto Him who saved me at such tremendous cost. ' Christ died, rose, and revived, that He might be Lord.' That He might be not only my Saviour, but my Sovereign. *Those who repeat ' I believe,' must go on to say, ' I belong,'* till over every realm and sphere of life you will write ' not my own.' Christ died to ' redeem us from all iniquity,' and ' a-l-l ' spells *all*, and means *all*. Does it mean that I may be delivered from all known sin here and now ? Yes, the moment I claim this full redemption God is true to His Word. But this *crisis* must be followed by a *process*. A photographer takes a likeness in a flash, but it has to go through a dark room that the image may be developed. That is what sanctification is—a crisis and a process. God gives us by His Spirit first grace to *see*, and then grace to cease —to see sin and to cease from it."

The speaker went on to dwell on " separation from the world, i.e. the separation of the Bride unto the Bridegroom. ' Christ redeemed us that we might receive the promise of the Spirit through faith.' Then the impossible becomes possible. Here is power to perform the divine purpose, God's dynamic to fulfil God's desire."

The same year two voices from afar bore messages to us— Pastor Rohrbach, from Berlin, and Rev. Edward Isaac, from Australia. The pastor referred to the letters on " The Practice of the Presence of God."—" An old book, but this Movement is old—as old as Pentecost, old as Elijah. Brother Lawrence, having to look after the fire and the food, could say, ' The presence of God fills my soul.' Covet the companionship of the Lord in daily life. When weary and tired I go to see a bed-ridden young woman, who keeps singing over and over,

> ' Count your blessings,
> Name them one by one.' "

Mr. Isaac, speaking of Christ as Lord, said : " Faith puts her hand into the hand of her Master, blindfold the while. Faith bears in her body the mark (stigma) of the Lord Jesus. Oh, to be willing to be stigmatics for Christ—not schismatics ; that is an unholy brand. What a difference between the self-advertising life that splutters and crackles to arrest attention, and the life that goes quietly on its heaven-borne way absorbed in the overmastering love of Jesus Christ."

The 1904 Report begins with a striking description of those who gathered to Keswick: " The Churchman and Nonconformist, the Conservative and the Liberal, the peer and the commoner, the followers of George Fox and of William Booth, the factory girl from the city slum and the child of delicate nurture and culture, the Bible-woman from the squalid court and the missionary from the Indian Zenana, the young graduate from the university, and the evangelist whose education has been of the most elementary character—all are attracted to the same spot that they may hear in their own tongue ' the wonderful works of God.' " This by F. B. M.

Another writer says : " It is impossible to refrain from a note of praise for the contribution which America has made to the blessed influence of the Convention "—Dr. Torrey as well as Dr. Pierson was amongst the teachers. Another refers to the fact that when one of the friends depended on for Bible Readings could not come, God supplied his place by a stranger (Dr. Torrey) at the eleventh hour.

And E. D., writing from Brighton, gives a summary of the teaching in words of Dr. George Wilson's. " Spirit-convicted disciples have been led to accept a Spirit-commended Christ, by a Spirit-generated faith, for a Spirit-assured victory, on the ground of a Spirit-formed Christ within." And adds a remark which thousands will echo. " If great blessing was found in the tents, let me say, for one at least, that as great a blessing was found within our home circle. It would be impossible to say how much we owed to our chaplain, beloved ' C. G. M.,' who morning by morning took the Word, and made it live, by opening some sweet spring of water which never failed us all the long bright day. A proverb of his had much wisdom in it : ' He that would enjoy the meetings, let him be happy in his home.' The social side of Keswick does in concentrated form what the tents do in a general way—it ministers a disposition to be Christlike. In our ' home ' I was living in the eighth of Romans all the time ; and some of the joy, which mingles in the sorrow of human parting, is, that I, by the indwelling Christ, can take this atmosphere back to Brighton with me."

One of the sermons was by the Rev. (now Archdeacon) Gresford Jones. " Of all tears," says John Bunyan, " they are the best that are made by the blood of Christ." It is as you and I catch a glimpse of the divine glory of the Atonement, that we then melt afresh in our hearts, and wonder at the love of God ; as this floods our hearts, there is born in us an irrepressible hunger to give out what we possess. It is not, Need I ? or May I ? or Must I ? but simply, How dare I not ? All over the country earnest souls are looking for a true lead and a strong lead—they look to you. May this be a week of renewed conviction and power overflowing to one another in love. May we draw down the fulness of the Spirit by the oneness of our longing for Him. On the mountain, or by the lake, in our room, or in the tent, may we have the vision, the reality of which one speaks—God and my own soul."

We dare not even touch the masterly Bible Readings of Dr. Pierson on Wisdom, Righteousness, Sanctification, Redemption, and of Dr. Torrey on The Personality of the Spirit, The Breath of God, The Spirit of Christ, and " Spirit of Burning come."

But there was one whose name begins to appear at this time, looked for ever since with eager expectancy. The Rev. Harrington Lees had learnt, perhaps from his former vicar, Mr. Brooke, a very interesting mode of comparing Scripture with Scripture. And from that day to this—as the remarkable attendance at his Bible Readings at Beckenham indicates—has been bringing forth out of his treasure things new and old. In 1904 he spoke on " ' The Lord will suddenly come to His temple.' ' The Lord whom ye seek,'—are we seeking Him ? " Then, speaking on Malachi iii. 2, " I was shown over a refinery. Metal melted down and passed from pan to pan, one-third left behind. ' What do you do with it ? ' ' We extract the silver from it.' Four words speak of the cleansing process—Fuller's soap, purging, i.e. sifting and straining, as in the gold diggings in Australia ; the refiner's fire and the purifying of metal ; its polishing to make permanent the reflection which before was but temporary All through 1890 God had been dealing with me. I knew not for what till one morning He gave me this promise, ' The Lord, whom ye grope for, shall suddenly come.' ' I am going to hold on, Lord,' I said, ' till Thou dost come.' When I came to Keswick all seemed darkness at first. Thank God the light came. Hold on to the Lord's promise and light will come for you."

That year, and many years, Prebendary Barnes Lawrence,

a man whose Hebrew Bible seems to be as much at his finger ends as his Greek Testament, had lessons for us never to be forgotten. " 'I am going home to the old scenes,' more than one has said to me; ' smoky chimneys of any manufacturing town are not like Keswick,' or ' the great London where I live is equally unlike.' Take for your comfort 1 Thessalonians v. 9–11. The Incarnation, Atonement, Ascension, Coming of the Holy Ghost, are that we SHOULD LIVE TOGETHER WITH CHRIST. It is not simply that we have a desire to live with Him. It is His desire to live with us. Long before He came, ' His delights were with the sons of men.' And when He came ' He ordained twelve '—to send them out to preach ? Yes, but first of all ' that they should be with Him.' And years after He said, ' I will not leave you orphans, I will come to you.' ' I and the Father will make our abode with the loving and obedient.' It is not for emergencies. It is for always : ' To me TO LIVE is Christ.' . . . Get down lower, lower, and you may take with you words just sung—

> ' He has entered ! He has entered !
> Every guest may now depart ;
> He has taken all the chamber
> Of my once divided heart.' "

Dr. Woelfkin spoke on the Priesthood of Christ. " A priesthood born out of double travail. The Epistle to the Hebrews says He must be a man tempted with all our temptations, and tried with all our heart-breaks. In Gethsemane and before it, it seemed as though Christ was crushed with depression, and caught in the cyclone of grief. So He woos our confidence by His sympathy."

The Ministers'. Meetings that year were times of peculiar power. Dear Mr. Brash unbosomed himself, telling us the story of God's dealings with him, and spoke of the result being a " blessed, real vivid sense of Christ always near, making it easy to draw on Him for each moment's need, and to throw oneself back on Him to do all."

Dr. Cumming spoke of the minister's power, " in the Word," " in the Spirit," and " in trust that every want for every hour will be supplied."

Next day Dr. Wilson spoke of the difficulties of pulpit and

parish work. " There must be no tricks " either in sermon or other work. Power to help struggling souls is according to the measure in which we are self-emptied and filled with God.

The Rev. E. W. Moore said : " Power for ministry is always the result of Christ's breathing on us and of our receiving the Holy Ghost."

Mr. Inwood on Thursday spoke from " He maketh His ministers a flame of fire," quoting Zinzendorf, " *I have but one passion—it is He.*"

Dr. Torrey closed this wonderful series of meetings on Friday by some keen home-thrusts. " A minister has unbounded ability to make or mar a church. Any minister not bringing men to definite acceptance of a definite Saviour is a failure. But besides this, we must feed the flock of God. Put no poison in the food. Never utter a word until you have found it true in the white light of God's presence. It is good to be honest, but it is best to be sure. Don't be frightened at being called saints ; it is a good word. If this is to be so, we must put out of our lives every known sin." The saddest confessions he had ever heard were from ministers. We must give up every doubtful thing, and even things right in themselves if they injure others. We need every ounce of power with everybody. We must have absolute consecration to God.

The chronicler of these meetings, J. R. M., speaks of the account as very imperfect ; but it brings back very vividly the memory of times of exceptional blessing.

Doctor John Smith, of Edinburgh, snatched from us in mid-career, was one from whom great help was expected. Another—long may *he* be with us—is Prebendary Webster. His facile pen depicts such scenes as that among the fisher folk described by an ardent Highlander. His ringing voice arouses the listener in church or tent. Speaking in 1901 of sunrise, he said: " I know it is a spiritual fact that when the Sun of Righteousness shines into a human heart, it brings health. The sunrise is instantaneous. The golden Orb darts over the snow-capped hills, and at once you feel the healing of the wings of light. Has there been a sunrise upon your soul ? Though Christ is in Heaven, yet, like the sun thousands of miles away, by His beams He can visit your soul. And when He comes, He comes to heal. Will you have this healing to-night ? "

CHAPTER XVII

"THE FEAST OF THE SEVENTH MONTH"

(AFTER THE REVIVAL IN WALES)

"During the great Durbar at Delhi a rich Indian prince had a plot of land allotted to him. It was a beautiful thought on his part to pay a large sum, that that plot might be free from taxes for ever; 'for,' said he, a 'king has rested there.' Even so the land which we have just surveyed, so burdened of yore, has been freed from its every encumbrance, because the King rested there."

REV. HARRINGTON LEES.

THE Keswick Convention is always in the seventh month and always a feast. But as we sit at the King's table on earth, we cannot but think of those who are feasting in heaven. Of none is this more so than of dear Robert Wilson, co-founder with Canon Battersby of this great Conference. Many looking in his face, with the light upon it bright as ever, but with signs of weakness beneath the light, must have said to himself as the century closed, "Thou shalt be missed, for thy place shall be empty." For five years this might have been said to him by visitors like Mr. Meyer, who sought him out at Broughton Grange. But now in 1905, "he was not, for God took him." A great company of saints laid him in the quietest of quiet graveyards, and multitudes have reason to thank God that he lived to do so manful a work for Broughton, for Keswick, and for England.

The previous autumn another and younger saint, with no premonitory symptoms of decay, had been taken from us to be for ever with the Lord. Caroline Head (*née* Hanbury), like Mr. Wilson, was of Quaker stock, her grandmother remaining in the Society of Friends through all her 108 years. But her father had joined the Church of England, and in its Evangelical circle her life opened like a beautiful flower. A sweet biography tells how that flower was watered by the truths of the deepening of the spiritual life when first they were restated.

147

Her sun never stood still, but went gloriously on,[1] and shone brighter still, when, in a home of her own, as Mrs. Albert Head, she had full scope for her influence. Those of us who remember social and spiritual gatherings in the house at Mildmay, and later in that at Richmond, were prepared for the unique influences exercised afterwards at Keswick. These only ceased with her translation to glory which took place on October 26, 1904. Tributes to both these beloved friends were borne at the opening meetings by Dr. Cumming and the Rev. E. W. Moore.

The same evening Mr. Inwood spoke on another theme. This was the year of the Welsh revival, and in common with many, Mr. Inwood had been deeply stirred thereby. " I can never again," he said, " be content with the ideals that in some measure satisfied me up to the time that I went to Wales. . . . We want a Convention in which the pressure of the Spirit of God is so overwhelming, that whole congregations go down before the Spirit. I believe that *that* is God's ideal, and, I pray you to ask God to lure you to the very best that He can do. Pray for the platform, that God will silence us, if He cannot speak through us ; that we may go out in passionate, Christlike, world-embracing longing for every child of God to be filled with the Spirit. We want a tidal wave that will take hold of everybody, and lift them clear into the harbour of full salvation. What that will mean for England God alone can tell. Do not let plans limit the Holy Spirit in this Convention ; do not plan even a copy of a Welsh revival. Give the Holy Spirit free way. Possibly the Convention may get out of our hands, but it will not get out of the hands of the Spirit. Shall our hearts say, Melt us down, break the meeting into pieces, that Jesus Christ may get the utmost glory in this Convention, for His Name's sake ? "

It is to be feared that these aspirations were only partially fulfilled. No doubt there were enormous meetings and admirable addresses. One might call attention to that of a new speaker, Archdeacon Madden, on " The Fulness of God," and of one of our best known speakers, the Rev. Evan Hopkins, on " Being filled with the Holy Ghost." " Whilst every man is born into the world with an evil *nature*, no one is born with

[1] See page 16 of present volume.

an evil *habit*. A habit is something that you wear. Take off the evil habit then ; lay it aside. If you lay aside a weight, it drops. This is God's way towards that fulness of the Spirit we desire. Then believe in order to receive. You may never really have honoured the Spirit as God. Put everything into His hands. You have often brought all but one or two things. ' That is such a little chamber, such a little drawer, I want to keep that key.' Nay, you are the Spirit's home, and He wants to walk through every part of your being, possessing, ruling, using, satisfying you. The soul that is filled with the Holy Ghost does not *feel* filled, there is no self-sufficiency. Many think, ' If I get the fulness of the Spirit, I shall have plenty of power, wisdom, and a very easy time.' Well, the full life *is* the easy life. ' My yoke is easy.' But ease comes by believing, by having your emptiness met by His fulness. If the cleansing and the separation from hindrances have been right up to your light, then the Holy Ghost *has* come—he *has* possessed you. Go forth and praise Him, trusting Him to use you."

Bible Readings by Prebendary Webb-Peploe and Mr. Brooke led us to the hills of frankincense. An address by the Rev. J. R. Macpherson made clear the difficult passage, " Whosoever sinneth hath not seen Him " (1 John iii. 6), and " He that doeth evil hath not seen God " (3 John 11). "What are we to make of it ? That whosoever lives in sinful habit of thought, or desire, *has never seen God in the real way* in which He desires to reveal Himself ? " Touching on Hebrews xii. 10, " That we may be partakers of His holiness," Mr. Macpherson said : " It is as if God came and sat down beside you, and drawing you to Himself said, I do not tell you to *go* and live a holy life ; I say *come* and let us do it ; you and I shall be partners in it. In the tight corners of life God gives us His own holiness ; any height of holiness we might reach at Keswick would never last if it were our own. But God's holiness will last, nay, will become pervasive, more absolute for daily life."

Another Church of Scotland man followed, the Rev. John Sloan. " Satan is saying, It is easy to trust God here, but when you leave, and friends leave you, and sinful or objectionable people surround you, it will be hard. Well, trust God to keep you trusting, and our faith will prove a victory that overcometh the world. I remember the moment and the spot where I learned to swim. A lot of us lads were in the water tumbling about like fishes. I recollect thrusting myself out to get over a wave, and I found that I had trusted the water, and that it was able to bear me up. When you trust Christ you will find that He can keep you from sinking."

Dr. Pierson was with us in great power from first to last. Speaking on 1 Thessalonians v. 18, etc., he said : " This is the only place in the Bible in which seven spiritual frames are put before us : ' Rejoice evermore '—the joyful frame ; ' pray without ceasing '—the prayerful frame ; ' in everything give thanks '—the thankful frame ; ' quench not the Spirit '—the watchful frame ; ' despise not prophesyings '—the teachable frame ; ' prove all things ; hold fast that which is good '— the judicial frame ; ' abstain from every form of evil '—the hallowed frame."

But there is a later address of Dr. Pierson's more likely to be remembered, for it told of a memorable meeting that had taken place the night before, a meeting which lasted till three o'clock in the morning. " When we proposed to gather in the tent for prayer it was obvious that there was some disturbing element—with remarks accusative and violent sounding like anarchy, and causing distress amongst those jealous for our harmony here. But a few prayed that God would overrule what was felt to be a Satanic disturbance. Feeling that the Spirit would have me speak, I ascended the platform and said : We are feeling desirous of an all-night meeting, but there are many people in this vicinity, some aged, some invalided, all in need of sleep. If you are content with a meeting till three in the morning I will stay with you ; thus let us not look on our own things, but on the things of others. If you will agree to that, raise your hands. Every hand went up, and the obvious difference between the conditions in that assembly before and after, showed Satan defeated and the Holy Ghost reigning.

" There were 368 written petitions for prayer. Most of them having two or three requests upon them ; these intercessions occupied an hour and a half. Confessions of sin followed—all sorts from all quarters, the tent meanwhile filling up to about seven or eight hundred. Then testing their trust in God, in response to a word from me, one rose and another, until every man and woman stood to claim God's fidelity to His promise.

"The hush of God came upon us. A man had come in, in a state of drink; he found Christ in the meeting, and going out brought in his wife with her babe and her sister. Friends laboured with these two women to bring them to the knowledge of Christ.

"One man that was prayed for is a minister of a church in England, and when the statement was read he got up and said : ' You may change to praise, for I am here and have got blessing ! ' And so, when it came to be twenty-five minutes to three, it was suggested that then it would be a good time to acknowledge in praise what God had done for us ; and just as we had had a marvellous witness of people rising to claim the power of God by faith, we had now another exhibition of people rising to testify in praise to God for blessing then and there received."

Friends at the Convention cannot be too thankful to God for putting it into Dr. Pierson's heart, in spite of weariness to go to this meeting, and then for giving him grace to pour oil upon the troubled waters. They *were* troubled, the torrent from the Welsh hills meeting the sluggish stream of English propriety threatened tumult. No doubt this was in the hope of extending to England the revival which had blessed Wales. That that hope might not be quenched one or two further meetings were arranged in which our Welsh friends had free play for their enthusiasm. Still it is to be feared that some disappointed feeling remained amongst them, for the attendance at the Convention in 1906 was three hundred less, being just the number that came from Wales in 1905, and—and this is sadly significant—a revival in England still remains conspicuous by its absence. Probably when it does come, as we believe it will, it will have its own character—not that of another nation ; and perhaps it may enter by another door, not by our Convention.

Writing of 1906, S. M. N. says : " There seemed nothing eventful this year as compared with the last ; no wave of confession and humiliation, no special moment, like that when the ' precious ' things were offered at the Ladies' Meeting, but there was a deeper, intenser tone. The great missionary meeting of Saturday had to be divided. We longingly hope many new recruits, chosen by the Lord, will go forth from this week."

Good work in other places was told about. Canon Barnes-Lawrence told of revival in two parishes. He was very urgent for personal holiness, practical holiness, holiness in the home, in the market, in business, holiness that *men* mark, above all a holiness that pleases God.

Dr. Harry Guinness spoke of the divided heart. He told of the first testimony he bore. A man in a medical meeting had said something of Christ that made his blood boil. Young Guinness found himself standing on his feet and addressing the President, Mr. (now Sir Frederick) Treves. He protested against " words concerning One who is my Lord, my Saviour, and my King. I sat down, not knowing whether there would be hissing or what. There was a thunder of applause ; and at the end Mr. Treves said to me, ' Come to these meetings, and if a man does what that man did to-night, do exactly as you did. I am very glad to meet you.' So," said Dr. Guinness, " if you are going to make Christ King, run up the flag."

Rev. Stuart Holden compared some who came to spectators in Alpine hotels, sitting on the verandah watching the climbers ascending beautiful peaks, yet never setting out to make any ascent themselves. " Don't let us be gazers, but climbers of these heights of holiness."

Mr. Hopkins spoke of the inconsistency of the new man going on wearing the clothes of the old man.

Dr. Griffith Thomas said, " No one who has attended the meetings of the Keswick Convention can ever be the same again, his life will be either the better or the worse." It was a solemn thought enforced in an able sermon at St. John's.

Another preacher there was the Rev. Stanton Jones. " Is there one here to-night," he said, " on whom the loveliness of Jesus has not yet dawned, or one sin-stained heart that needs the pierced hands ; he has passed through spiritual conflict here, and reached no peace, no calm, no holy rest. Oh, that the light of the knowledge of the glory of God might break in upon you in the face of Jesus Christ."

Mr. Webb-Peploe gave Bible Readings on the Four Gospels. Dr. Campbell Morgan on the Lord's Prayer. What new heights and depths he showed us in the familiar words !

On Thursday afternoon, the day when the crowded train

from Barrow and elsewhere brings its hundreds, the Rev. S. A. Selwyn spoke from Isaiah xxxi. 6–9, " Turn ye unto Him from whom the children of Israel have deeply revolted," etc. " How miserably few are the conversions in our churches and chapels to-day. And what about ourselves ? Have we been loyal to the Lord Jesus Christ ? Or is there a controversy between us and God ? Such keeping back renders one useless in the Master's service. The Lord claims our allegiance in the home. ' Business must be attended to,' and it shuts out family prayers. Where does the King's business come in ? "

Speaking of the love of God Mr. Selwyn pointed in contrast to many a church to-day as a desperately cold North-Pole sort of place. " . . . Some of us are afraid of the fire of God. What happened when those Hebrew captives were flung into the burning fiery furnace ? It burned their bonds. Are you afraid of the Holy Ghost doing that ?

> ' Oh, for a love which loves unto death !
> Oh, for a fire that burns ! ' "

The following year was marked by a unique meeting, a Reception of our fellow-subjects from the Colonies, and of our fellow-Christians from foreign lands. Bishop Ingham, Preb. Webb-Peploe and Mr. Hopkins greeted them. Response was made by Baron Nicolai. There were other Russians there, and, thank God, they were side by side with Japanese. As we broke up a venerable Swedish pastor said : " I came to England for the Evangelical Alliance ; my host pressed me to stay ; I stayed, and I have seen Westminster Abbey, I have seen Windsor Castle, and now *best of all* I have seen the Keswick Convention."

The Bible Readings were in the delightful hands of the Rev. Hubert Brooke, and of Dr. Pierson, who took for his subjects, *Unsubdued sin, Unanswered prayer, Persistent darkness*, and *Habitual unbelief*.

Mr. Brooke, speaking of the controversy on perfection, pointed to Hebrews v. 14, where the same word is used as in Hebrews vi. 1. In the one case it is translated " full age," in the other " perfect." " You do not give strong meat to little babes but to full-grown people. The very fact that we are born into the Kingdom of God implies that we are to grow,

L

and that to the full stature that our life is capable of.
This is what we are to aim at, this is Christian perfection."

Dr. Pierson, speaking on unanswered prayers said solemnly :
"The majority of prayers are unanswered. St. James gives
the reasons. In i., lack of faith and patience. In iv., selfishness
and worldly alliance. In v., lack of importunity and lapsing
from the level of faith. But over against this set the fact
that some people do pray and get answers. Two generations
ago George Müller raised a monument to a prayer-hearing
God, and the acids of the atmosphere have not worn it
away. When he died people said, 'Who knows Mr.
Wright ?' But the work went on. And when *he* died
people said, 'No one knows Mr. Bergin,' yet the last report
shows larger answers to prayer than ever."

Mr. Harrington Lees, speaking on Mark ii. 12, said : "A
great purpose of our Convention is for paralysed souls, to
teach them how to walk. They say Keswick teaches quietism.
Where was the quietism in the story of the paralytic ? That
was when the man lay there paralysed. What we teach here
is the blessed quietism of God's power."

In another address he said, "We hear much about Christian
conflict, but surely that should be a campaign not a mutiny—
warfare against sin, not rebellion against God." Speaking
of victory he said : "People say it is like a mirage in the desert.
We see our calling, the city, the oasis, the trees, the fruit,
but when we get nearer all is gone. Not so : if you keep walking in the Spirit. As Isaiah xxxv. 7 says R.V. (marg.), 'The
mirage shall become a pool.'"

The Rev. E. W. Moore gave a beautiful illustration of a
vessel unto honour. He recalled Bernard Palissy; he took
us to the Vatican, with its vases of malachite, alabaster and
porcelain. "But as far as I could perceive they could serve
no useful purpose. God has no vessels to honour which are
not useful. Cleanse the inside of the cup, then Christ can
fill it with the pure water of life. God wants clean vessels
for holy ministries, and (changing the figure) Christ is making
up His legion of honour. When His roll is called up yonder,
will you be there ? "

This was followed by silent prayer broken by the Chairman,

Captain Tottenham, starting the chorus, "When the roll is called up yonder, I'll be there."

A striking address was that of Pastor Findlay. "Many have come from places where they have little spiritual help, or fellowship, and tremble at going back to such surroundings. But Christ says, ' Lo, I am with you all the days.' The Lord will do wonders. He Himself will be with you in your trying circumstances, your parched land, your place of drought. Others of you who were here twelve months ago, and went back full of joy, and power, and thought you had nothing before you but a glorious time, now you come back with broken hearts, for there has been failure, failure, failure. Well, the Lord will do wonders for you. You cannot carry the tent and its surroundings with you, but you can take Him with you everywhere, and there is not a spiritual blessing you can long after but God is ready to give."

We should like to quote an address of the Rev. John Sloan, but can only pick out this : "A lady in spiritual difficulty, to everything her minister could say, replied, Oh, I cannot trust Him. ' What has Jesus done that you cannot trust Him ? ' he replied. And in a moment the light broke in. Venture out into the deep to-night. Put yourself, your interests, concerns, prospects, failures, sins—leave them all with Him, and say I will trust and not be afraid."

The Rev. E. L. Hamilton : " May all of us know experimentally what it is to be born again and to dwell in the Kingdom of God. If we are in that Kingdom it is only reasonable we should keep its laws and principles. It is the best way to extend His Kingdom, and the only way to get its riches and blessings." And then he went on to lead us into some of the secrets of the Sermon on the Mount. And speaking of a common temptation, he said, "Thank God there is salvation from it, salvation at the place called Calvary."

The Rev. Ernest Dowsett : " Though I had all I wanted once, a happy home, a beautiful church, a loving people, I was thirsty still. But from the smitten Rock came water that satisfied. Ankle-deep life is a miserable business. Be knee-deep, loin deep : nay, find the waters to swim in. People say, ' You will never be able to live up to it.' But this Water—it is not like the fountain in Trafalgar Square—' shall be in you ' and that will sustain your life."

CHAPTER XVIII

"THE BANKS OF ULAI"

"Yes. There are greener pastures, stiller streams,
And music baffling all life's mortal dreams;
Lead on, then, Shepherd Lord, new glory waits,
Ambushed in shadow by yon sunset gates."

C. A. Fox.

THE outstanding event of 1909 (the next year under review), was the visit of the revered Bishop of Durham, and especially his address to ministers. It had been our privilege in the garden-house at Addlestone, where Mr. and Mrs. Hopkins gather a group of friends in the spring, to suggest that, as Dr. Moule had kindly promised to come to Keswick, he should be asked to give an address at a ministers' meeting. It was difficult to arrange. The Bishop had to return to Durham the night of the first ministers' meeting, but he lingered to speak to us, and surely none that heard him will ever forget the "thrilling and tender tones in which he developed his theme (from 2 Cor. iv. 6), the shining of the heavenly radiance within, with a view to the diffusion of the light of the knowledge of the glory of God in the face of Jesus Christ."

" A pastor exercising his pastorate amiss may make untold unhappiness, unrest, all that is undesirable to an extent that cannot be measured . . . while the man who forgets himself and carries the Lord Christ about with him in his life and into his ministry, though he may not have brilliant gifts, may be a centre of untold blessing in the Master's hands. God hath shined into our hearts to give the light of the knowledge of the glory of God, i.e., with a view to the illuminating diffusion of God's glory; God has lit the light in the lantern not merely to light *it*, but to light the darkness around. There has been kindled a spark of glory in these hearts of ours; it shows us the darkness first no doubt, but the prevalent thought is the

thought of what is luminous and beautiful and of the eternal
day. Servant of God, man of God, messenger of God, ask
that by the power of the Spirit there may be made manifest
Christ in His manifold yet harmonious glory—The Lamb of
Calvary, the Prince of Life, and the Light of the Celestial
City." " The Lord Christ left the tomb empty to its inner-
most corner. He left it for His session and intercession above.
Ask for a large light upon that in your pastoral heart and then
for illumination on the fair face of the Bridegroom Who is
coming again—for without a to-morrow, we cannot live rightly
to-day."

All this must have stirred into flame the gift in many a
minister and missionary ; still more perhaps when Dr. Moule
spoke of *Christ in the heart*—" *there in residence,* in the study,
in the pulpit, in the parish. We have to talk about many
things. We have to be men with men, understanding many
a problem ; but we are not to scatter our ministry so as ever
to let it be doubtful that the burden of the Lord, laden with
the gold of the everlasting hills, is the glory of God in the face
of Jesus Christ. I had ambitions "—and here spoke the
Fellow of Trinity—" to preach about many things, but now
I feel that I have nothing to preach about save the Lord Jesus
Christ. I am certain that we shall be driven upon that subject
next Saturday, when the miners and their families are expected
to crowd Durham Cathedral. What is more, I believe there
is nothing else they would so wish me to talk about. They
talk of other things amongst themselves, things in which they
know well they have our sympathies, but if *we* try thus to
talk—without, perhaps, the knowledge of experts—we shall
fail. Nay, let us remember that we are God's messengers
to men's souls. So God hath shined into our hearts, that we
may give out the light to other men ; therefore, for our beloved
people's sake, let us covet a glorious Christ for ourselves."

Very different was the minister's meeting of the next year.
Yet we are not sure but that it was as remarkable. No other
that we have attended recalled more vividly the time of testimony in Oxford. After a very lucid statement from the
Chairman (Rev. Evan Hopkins), putting the theology of the
teaching in terse clear sentences, testimonies were asked for,
especially from one seated by the Chairman. It was a very

sacred revelation, and it would at once mar the beauty of such a narration, and ill-requite the self-crucifixion which prompted it, for another to attempt to detail it in print. Suffice it to say that the speaker, who, until so lately, knew no form of Christian life but that of Ritualism extreme, begged us to remember that men so ranked were many of them no mere formalists. However, their plan of salvation had not brought him deliverance, nor satisfied his yearning for blessing among his flock. One of his parishioners told him of Keswick, and two years ago he came. Very isolated he felt, and there was much in our methods to " get over." A conversation with the chairman brought light, and such as he had he gave his people. Last year he came again, and now it was personal failure that troubled him. He felt at first that he could not forego what had been so dear, but, when grace came to renounce it, joy and peace came in. Returning home he felt that he must start a prayer-meeting ; but how could he dare. Besides would any one come ? When he arrived he found the prayer-meeting already started. What a greeting ! And when he had down a mission preacher from the Evangelization Society, and subsequently another for children, when at these missions whole families were brought in—ninety souls in all in the village—what reason was there to thank God and take courage !

Two names stand out pre-eminently amongst our teachers in 1910, Mr. Goforth and Mr. Gordon. Mr. Goforth took us across the world to learn lessons from those who are but little children in the faith. He showed us that " everywhere in China, sin hindered God, sin hindered prayer ; and how, when sin was confessed, aye and restitution made, prayer flowed in like a torrent. At one great meeting in Honan, a man, trembling and in tears, said : ' Brother Chen, I've been saying things behind your back to lower your reputation, forgive me, for my heart is breaking over it.' ' Brother,' said Mr. Chen, ' that is all swept away, mention it never again.' That man made restitution, and so could pray with power. Keep right on petitioning, and keep right on praising. The Bible is full of thanksgiving. May God use the poor, ignorant Koreans to provoke us to jealousy, to repent and pray and praise. Dr. Chapman heard an Irishman praying ' Lord Jesus, I give up everything that I may have the promise of the Father. I have done all that I can do, and I expect Thee to do all that THOU canst do. By faith I receive God the Holy Spirit.' Within six months he had led sixty-eight to Christ."

Multitudes in London and elsewhere remember with joy the visit of Mr. S. D. Gordon. He was a great power at Keswick, too. " The Lord Jesus," he said, " drew men to Himself. That was what He was after, the personal touch between men and Himself. All service that is worth while grows out of this. It was through the human life of the divine Jesus that the Holy Spirit began His work. Christ stayed here but a short time, and covered a small area, but He sent the Holy Spirit upon us and we are to follow, doing what He did, and living His life albeit, in a secondary way.

" I have spoken of one group of experiences as the warp, another as the dark threads, and a third as the bright threads that shuttle across the warp, and driven in by the weaver's beam make up the pattern of life ; so our Master calls us to follow Him. If there were the sovereignty of the Holy Spirit, there would be a Pentecost of which that in the Acts was but a beginning. I hardly know how to pack my words. If we lived Christ our lips might be dumb ; if we lived Christ there would be a wondrous change in the world. The world does not want Bibles bound like this (and it is good binding), it wants Bibles bound in shoe leather. Teachers of whom I have made idols showed that they had feet of clay, the life was so much less than the teaching that I almost stumbled. Then I went alone and said, ' Master, Thou art true.' Jesus lived what He taught, and, as a missionary from India said, if we gave the Bible to the Hindoos and *lived* it, the rest would all come. True for India, and for our lands too."

1911 " was an all-British Convention as far as the platform was concerned." Dr. Pierson had been invited, but God had called him home. How we missed him, and miss him still !

The numbers were excellent, especially the number of men. Seventy in the Cambridge Camp, and, writes F. S. W., " at a prayer-meeting there, nearly all took part." Two houses were filled with Oxford men, and eighteen Chinese students were present.

A new feature was the holding unofficial meetings for Scottish, Welsh, and Irish attendants; the two former on two occasions in the Victoria Hall; "the Irish contingent in a garden party arranged by Miss Bradshaw, and addressed by Canon Douse, the Revs. W. Baillie, and R. Northridge."

There were four Bishops at Keswick, and also the new Pastor at the Tabernacle, Dr. Dixon, and the C.M.S. Secretary, the Rev. Cyril Bardsley.

"As speakers for the first time," says F. S. W., " we had the Rev. H. L. C. V. de Candole, of Cambridge, the Rev. C. W. Wilson, of St. James', Holloway, and the Rev. Dundas Harford."

The chronicler goes on to refer to the Bible Readings of Dr. Campbell Morgan and Mr. Harrington Lees, and to other addresses recorded in the Keswick Week; and then he says this, " the angels' day-books contain many a story of sacred scenes in the churchyard, on the Castle Hill, by the side of the lake, where wounded children of God were helped to get back into touch with Jesus Christ."

The Rev. Cecil Wilson in an address on personal friendship with Christ said, "How is it that your hearts and mine do not thrill more at the very thought of it ? Christ cannot give that wonderful personal friendship unless we are prepared to let nothing stand in its way." And he added, " we do not do the most when we are bustling about and rushing round, we need to be still to know Him."

The Rev. Hector Mackinnon—alas, so soon to be snatched away from us—speaking on growth in grace, said, " Many people are far more concerned about the vineyards of others than their own." Then he proceeded to expound the classic of sanctification, Romans vi. " When we speak of going with Christ to the grave, that is correct if we have been previously with Him to the Cross and died upon it. We become dead to the power of sin by the exercise of the same faith in the same Person, and lie upon the same Cross, by the exercise of which we became dead to the penalty of sin. Sanctification is possible because it is all in Christ, whose love can flow into your soul and mine in such fulness that victory will sit at our right hand."

In 1912 we had many of the veterans with us and not a few recruits. Among the latter were the Rev. Herries Gregory, the able son of an able father, and Mr. Daniel Crawford, the most unconventional of Convention speakers. Everyone missed Preb. Webb-Peploe, absent through illness, and Dr. Meyer, who had been full of fire and energy the year before. It was good to welcome back the Rev. Hubert Brooke, of whom illness then deprived us. And it was indeed a puzzle to know whether to listen to his wit and wisdom, or to go to the other tent and hear Dr. Dixon discourse on the Incarnation.

Very earnest and able were words spoken by some of our sisters. We can refer to only one. At a gathering of missionaries, 270 in number, Mrs. Head said " the missionary often has to say, ' How busy I am,' but always should add, ' How near God is,' and (quoting Dr. Lawes), ' I would sometimes give up, but that I remember, God lives, and my father is praying.' Let us who are at home so act that many a missionary may say, ' God lives, and some one is praying.' " Mr. Crawford followed in prayer, one sentence of which was " Oh ! the solemnity of being walking and talking Bibles, whom the heathen are reading."

Bishop Ingham preached a striking sermon next day from " My Father worketh hitherto, and I work," or, he said, giving a modern rendering, " My Father worketh unceasingly, and so do I." On the Monday evening the Rev. Stuart Holden gave one of the most striking and timely of addresses. " There is to-day," he said, " in faith's name, a recrudescence of seeking for signs from Heaven, signs which when granted have little to identify them with the simplicity of Christ. When God's children can be led to think that incoherent gibberings and physical contortions (often leading to immorality) are of God, beware of anything and of any one that comes to you as an angel of light, with that which is alien to the simplicity of Christ." These warnings ought to be printed separately.

It is safe to say that the raciest address ever heard at Keswick was that of Mr. Crawford, for twenty-three years missionary of " the land of the long grass," as he called Central Africa. It was good to know that it was at Keswick that the call to this unique service came. " When God said to me *here*. ' Go,' I spoke to Hudson Taylor about plunging a thousand miles into the jungle, and he said : ' The worst of it is, if you do, you may be shut in,' but then he added beautifully : ' They may shut you in, but they cannot roof you in.' Here you trot out a pretty little phrase about ' daily bread,' and lay in provisions for a month ; but the prayer is a very real one in Africa. We write in charcoal on our walls, ' The God of Eternity is the God of this hour.' We are on apostolic ground, and don't ask in what ecclesiastical pill-box a man is shut up. Our Bibles often give us telegrams from glory. A chief spat in my face, and this flashed along the wire, ' They spat in His face,' and then this ' From Whose face the earth and heaven fled away.' "

Just one word of the very powerful addresses of Dr. Dixon must suffice. " Time was," said Luther, " when seeing temptation, I said, ' Lord, there is a fight on hand ; Lord help me ;' and the devil whipped me every time. Now I say, ' Lord, there he is, at him for me,' and down he goes."

Instead of quoting further from addresses, let us try for once—it will be in special keeping with the title of this chapter—to initiate our readers into the delights of the praise meeting at seven on Saturday morning. The meeting of this year, 1912, was by no means exceptional. It simply evinces the spirit of praise in which, in fair weather or foul, the great congregation gathers for a parting blessing. The scene is probably indescribable to one who has never witnessed it, but one may recall a few of the sentences that held us in joyful hope for an hour or more. When the Chairman called for words of testimony, one sprang to his feet saying, " Thou hast girded me with gladness." Another, " Sin shall not have dominion over you." A third, " By the help of my God I will leap over the wall."

When testimonies as well as texts were permitted, one exclaimed, " I prayed the Lord to fill me with His Spirit, and I believe He has." Another, " God has blessed me and I am going forth in His strength to live it out." Another, " I have had clearer vision of the Lord Jesus as my All-sufficient Saviour from the power of sin." Another, " My insufficiency but God's sufficiency." Another, " I have fallen in love with Keswick, but still more with Keswick's Lord." " There is a re-adjustment between this body and its Creator and Redeemer." " I shrink from the cross, but I have proved ' no cross, no

crown.' " " The garment of praise for the spirit of heaviness.
I've got it." And the happy audience could not repress a
sympathetic smile.

A large company stood up together and repeated, " Of His
fulness have all we received."

The leader of a band of nine said, " Here are the nine. And
we want to say, we will bless the Lord from this time forth and
for evermore."

Another large party, " ' Go your way, eat the fat and drink
the sweet, and send portions to them for whom nothing is
prepared.' We are a party of twenty from the colliery district.
God is working in Barnsley as in *Down in Water Street* or in
Broken Earthenware."

When the platform was reached Mr. Hopkins led us and
other ministers followed. There Lord Radstock said, " The
government shall be upon His shoulder." Mr. Martin Sutton,
" I am here for the first time. The Lord is in this place and I
knew it not." Mr. Budd, " Is Thy God able to deliver thee
from the lions ? . . No manner of hurt was found in Daniel because he believed in his God." Mr. Crawford, " Twenty-four
years ago I went from Keswick to Africa, and have lived on
the truth you love. I have found, *not* after the cross the
crown, but that the cross *is* a crown. At that cross where
Satan did his worst, God did His best."

Another missionary said, " Why call ye Me Lord, Lord, and
do not the things that I say ? ' Go ye into all the world, and
preach the Gospel to every creature,' and that ' not where
Christ was known.' "

Miss Nugent gave us Luke vi. 17 and Ezekiel iii. 23. Mrs.
Hopkins, " Jesus showed Himself again unto His disciples."
A stranger rose and said, " I asked for the Holy Spirit ; God
has answered, and I am going to try and *take*, and I know that
He will *undertake.*"

For his own testimony Mr. Head read the three closing verses
of Ephesians iii., adding, " Let all the people say Amen." We
sang a verse of " All hail the power of Jesus' name," and
prayer by Bishop Cassells closed the meeting.

At the close of the Sunday evening services another praise
meeting, still more informal, is now a recognized institution.
One such meeting comes up before us in which the men of the

Oxford house, one after another, testified to God's grace given. Then rose a stalwart form from the officer's house. He spoke of blessings received there, one of the recipients having begun the week very far away from God.

But one must go to such a meeting to realize the intensity of heavenly delight and trust manifested thereat.

As we go to print, the Keswick Week 1913 comes to hand :—

This was a year which will be distinguished in the annals of Christian life in England by the Swanwick Conference. Three hundred delegates of the C.M.S. there met at the end of May to welcome home brethren who had paid a visit of enquiry to the far east. These brethren, whose hearts had been set upon development, had found on return a cry for retrenchment. But at Swanwick they met a large group of local secretaries. They prayed unitedly and at one time separately " for nearly an hour."

" Step by step the Holy Spirit led them " until on the last morning they stood up and unanimously passed the following resolutions :—

First—That we believed God was calling us to advance.

Second—To re-adjustment of habits, of expenditure, so that more money might be released for God's service.

Third—That there should be an appeal for an offering of a thousand individual gifts of £100 to the Society and an effort to increase regular contributions, from 25 to 50 per cent.

At a Committee Meeting at Zion College on July 8 there was only one message from every auxiliary, " Go forward." By that time £80,000 had been assured and it was felt—as in the earlier Conference— that of a truth the living God was amongst us. One who came in for a short time said, " I felt as if I had stepped into a chapter of the Acts." We began that meeting with the " Veni Creator," and we finished it with the " Te Deum." It is believed that other Societies have been inspired to follow this gracious example.

Keswick, always sensitive to spiritual movements, immediately felt the thrill of Swanwick, and many times during the Convention references were made to the holy gathering in that little Derbyshire town. It was a happy thought to ask the Rev. Cyril Bardsley, one of the apostles surely of that Pentecost, to be one of the preachers to inaugurate the Convention. And it was a happy thought of the preacher to make the events referred to the subject of his sermon. Indeed, more than one said to him, " There is only one subject you can take." He took it with " this dominant thought, that which has been going on, is not anything connected with the Church Missionary Society, so much as a movement affecting all home and foreign Missionary Societies, or, more truly still, the whole Church."

Our previous quotations are from that sermon, and we have only room to add Mr. Bardsley's urging us " to think about personal holiness not first for our own sake. Next, to think much about personal sacrifice.

Love of comforts amongst God's people can prevent us from doing our best possible for His work. Calvary *must* precede Pentecost. Lastly, think much of the greatness, glory, purpose of our God, and pray for a great faith. Our individual faith is too weak, hence our need of being heart to heart, mind to mind, so that our united faith may be strong enough to grasp God's promises."

Bishop Taylor Smith spoke wonderful words on the Monday evening. " Besides the Master and His disciples there is another speaker at Keswick, not an invited speaker at all, but one who will speak perhaps more often than those invited. I mean Satan. On the mountain side, and on the lake, in the lonely wood where you have gone apart from the world [in the Tent too], you will find Satan. He will speak, will go as far as to quote Scripture, but will stop in the middle of a verse. When he leaves his victims or would be victims, he leaves them to the wild beasts. But our Master never leaves, He will stay with us—is with us all the days—not only the days of Keswick, but the days which follow. . . . People say, ' Are you going to Keswick ? ' and add ' you will have a great blessing,' as though there were magic in the air and healing in the lake ; just as men might have said of old, ' Are you going to Bethesda ? ' and the man ill for thirty-eight years might have answered, ' I am, and I am expecting a great blessing ; in fact, I am hoping to be cured.' But friends, the blessing was not in the place, the blessing was in the Person. And only as we come into personal touch with the Lord Jesus shall we go away blessed. . . . Language fails to tell what God has in store for you. First the gift, then the victory, and then the winning of souls. That is the programme of Christianity."

It was good once more to see our old friend the Rev. George Grubb on the platform, now speaking of " Transformation by the indwelling Christ," and now telling of wondrous scenes in Australia, then of a wondrous woman in Russia, an ignorant woman who could not read was Katty and a drunkard to boot. But God saved her from drink and she felt she must learn to read for the sake of the New Testament. When she reached the Acts, she said, " Lord, those early Christians had something the people do not have now. What wonderful things they did when filled with the Spirit, and, dear Saviour, Thou hast saved me from drink, now, blessed Jesus, make me an early Christian." And He did in marvellous ways.

In Australia, he told of three Missions, and three Conventions in Sydney and other cities. And of a visit to the mining centre of Broken Hill, where " Mr. Jackson, Mrs. Grubb and I had meetings in the Methodist Church, the Baptist Church, the Presbyterian Church, the Salvation Army Citadel, the Church of Christ, and the Congregational Church. " So I defy any one to tell me what church I belong to. I find that God is no respecter of Churches. The only thing necessary in an individual or a church is to ' Draw nigh to God and He will draw nigh to you.' "

Prebendary Webb-Peploe gave Bible Readings on " The life which is life indeed "; and the Rev. Charles Inwood on " The transfigured life, and out and out Consecration."

" Apparently," writes Prebendary Webster, " Mr. Inwood's ecclesiastical status is not generally known, for the following conversation was overheard in the tent :—' Is he an Anglican ? ' ' I don't know ; but he is one of the best of them, if he is.' "

There were new voices heard this year. Our brothers Graham Scroggie, Russell Howden, and W. Y. Fullerton, were practically new at Keswick, and their messages were exceedingly valuable. Mr. Scroggie's address at the Friday prayer meeting on " Vision, Passion, Mission," was timely and illuminating.

Keswick owed great things to the C.M.S. meetings at Swanwick this year. In some previous years the C.M.S., as Mr. Eugene Stock shows in its History, owed not a little to Keswick. In 1887 Preb. Webb-Peploe and Mr. Johnson of Lagos, going to London from a glorious Keswick missionary meeting, pressed on the C.M.S., and successfully, " THE POLICY OF FAITH."

In 1890 a " Keswick letter," written from the Lakeside by earnest C.M.S. friends, asking for A THOUSAND MISSIONARIES in the next few years, led to additions of 800 by 1899, being three times the number of previous similar periods. " Not unto us, O Lord, not unto us, but unto Thy name be glory ! "

CHAPTER XIX

FORTY YEARS OF MERCIES

" I only pray that through the coming days
Of this my life unceasingly may steal,
Into some aching heart,
Strains that shall help to heal
Its long-borne pain, to lift the thoughts
From self and worldly gain,
To fill the life with harmonies divine.
Oh ! may such power be mine.
Thus would I live, and, when my work is o'er,
May the rich music of my life
Ring on for evermore."

THUS have we sought to glean and gather amongst the sheaves of these forty years of mercies.

It seemed best to keep with hardly an exception .(after the scenes of origin were described) to Keswick itself. But I must refer to a remarkable Conference at Norwich, where we speakers were disturbed by the hail that rattled on the glass roof of the place of assembly. Mr. Marcus Rainsford was there to help us with his rare gifts of exposition. Much later Mr. Middleton gathered convention after convention on Keswick lines in which God gave a great spirit of hearing.

At Manchester Conventions were repeatedly held, and monthly meetings gathered by that ardent Irishman, Mr. Leonard Shaw, made the Hall at Strangeways a centre whence radiated light and truth.

Time would fail to tell of Liverpool and Newcastle, of Carlisle and Nottingham, of Buxton and Harrogate, of Exeter and Weston-Super-Mare, of Folkstone, Margate and Ipswich, of Weymouth and Teignmouth and scores of other places, large and small. In or near the Metropolis, Bayswater, Ealing and Wimbledon have for years had an annual convention, and so has Blackheath, but that seems merged now in one at Woolwich.

The sainted Francis Paynter started an important convention at Guildford, at first in a tent, then in a beautiful Hall which he built. An energetic layman, Mr. Stratton has for years worked a convention in a large marquee at Melksham. It was beautiful to see the crowd gathered under the canvas to listen to a thrilling, touching address by Mrs. Bramwell Booth, but most of the speakers dealt with varied aspects of the subject of sanctification.

This enumeration is by no means complete and we must ask forgiveness if names of places as eager and alert as those named have been omitted. The list too consists wholly of English towns. Well, what about the Celtic fringe? Great gatherings at Glasgow, when Dr. Cumming was minister of Sandiford Parish, have been detailed upon an earlier page. But now we want to speak of another Scotch Convention much smaller but yet more representative.

> " On the Banks of Allan Water
> When the sweet spring time" doth "fall,"

not only residents but a goodly company of visitors have been wont to assemble year by year since 1892. The Convention originated in a meeting at Keswick in the previous year attended by a considerable number of Scotsmen who were present at that Convention. Mr. Robert Wilson, it is believed, occupied the Chair at the Bridge of Allan at the beginning.

Mr. R. H. Stewart of Hillfoot, Dumbartonshire, gives us this information and continues : " Mr. William Ferguson, LL.D., of Kinmundy, Aberdeenshire, who was perhaps the originator of the Bridge of Allan Convention, was the first Scotsman to act as its Chairman. On his decease in 1904 he was succeeded as chairman by Mr. Duncan McLaren, of Edinburgh, who still acts.

" The Rev. W. D. Moffat, M.A., of Edinburgh, acted as the first Convener of Committee from 1891 till 1908, when he resigned owing to advancing age and the increasing claims of his own work." He passed away in 1912. " The Rev. Hector Mackinnon, M.A., of Shettleston, Glasgow, was in 1908 appointed Convener, and acted as such till his death, in his early prime, in 1913, since which time I have acted as Secretary.

" The Convention was at first held in a tent seated for 2,000 persons. It was always too large, and the Convention was after some years transferred to a Hall holding about 800. Of recent years the Convention has been held in a tent seated for about 400, and holding about 600. The last Convention, that of 1913, was attended by about 400. These Bridge of Allan Conventions have been marked with much spiritual power and blessing."

Every reader of Lord Macaulay's History will remember his account of " The south-western part of Kerry, now well known as the most beautiful tract in the British Isles. The mountains, the glens, the capes stretching far into the Atlantic, the crags on which the eagles build, the rivulets brawling down rocky passes, the lakes overhung by groves in which the wild deer find covert, attract, every summer, crowds of wanderers sated with the business and the pleasures of great cities. . . . On the days when the sun shines out in all his glory, the landscape has a freshness and a warmth of colouring seldom found in our latitude. The myrtle loves the soil. The arbutus thrives better than even on the sunny shores of Calabria. The turf is of livelier hue than elsewhere ; the hills glow with a richer purple ; the varnish of the holly and ivy is more glossy ; and berries of a brighter red peep through foliage of a brighter green."

The crown and centre of this exquisite region is Killarney, and it was surely a happy thought to arrange for an Irish " Keswick " to be held annually in this spot. How it began and continues is contained in the following memorandum from Mr. Beale of Cork, countersigned by the Chairman, Mr. Crosbie, Ballyheigue :—

" About ten years ago I had a surprise visit (which gave me great pleasure) from Mr. John W. Leahy of South Hill, Killarney, and Mr. J. D. Crosbie, of Ballyheigue Castle, enquiring the addresses of some Keswick speakers with whom they could correspond, as they were desirous of starting a Convention on Keswick lines ; and I think it important to mention that previous to this a few earnest Christians in Killarney had been wont to meet weekly at a united prayer meeting, at which the Holy Spirit led the late J. W. Leahy, and the Rev. J. Hadden, Wesleyan Minister at Killarney, to seek, that the way might be opened for such a gathering.

M

" The answer followed in the holding of the first Killarney Convention in the fine dining-room of the Lake Hotel, by the kind permission of Mr. J. Hilliard, Proprietor.

" This Meeting took place in the third week of May, 1905. The Speakers were :—Captain Tottenham (Chairman), Rev. J. Stuart-Holden, Rev. Harrington Lees. Some extra chairs had to be requisitioned, the attendance being about 150.

" Much interest being evinced, the Committee subsequently ventured on hiring a tent, which was placed on the grounds of the Lake Hotel, which is about two miles from the town, and again a larger tent, and about two summers past the trustees with the kind help of friends purchased a new tent to accommodate about 800. At the last Convention this tent was comfortably filled at the night Meetings, as some came then from Tralee.

" It is comfortably seated, and lighted with electric light.

" Mr. J. W. Leahy took a great interest in these Meetings but his call ' Home,' happy for him, was a sad loss to our Committee.

" The local clergy in Killarney take an earnest interest in the Convention. The Bishop of Limerick has on several occasions taken part in the opening of a Meeting, and quite a large number of clergy of all denominations come from various parts.

" The visitors last year filled up the Lake Hotel and about six others in the neighbourhood.

" The following have taken part in succeeding years, some of them on more occasions than one : Rev. Evan H. Hopkins, Rev. Stuart Holden, Rev. Harrington C. Lees, Capt. Tottenham, Rev. Charles Inwood, Rev. Canon Barnes-Lawrence, Rev. R. C. Joynt, Rev. Hubert Brooke, Rev. J. Smyth Wood, Rev. W. Y. Fullerton, Rev. J. Chalmers Lyon, Rev. Hector Mackinnon, Rev. W. S. Standen.

" In addition, many missionaries from various mission fields have given short addresses on Missionary Day.

" Mr. and Mrs. Crawford and others spoke last year.

" The Convention is on Keswick lines and in care of seven trustees : Lord Langford, Capt. Wade-Thompson, Messrs. Alfred Beale, James D. Crosbie, W. H. Going, J. W. Martin, George F. Trench."

So, something has been done for a central Convention for each of the three kingdoms, nor would " gallant little Wales " consent to be left out. " Wales," says the polyglot George Borrow, " signifies a land of mountains, of vales, of dingles, chasms, and springs. It is a country in which nature displays herself in her wildest, boldest, and occasionally loveliest forms. Of remarkable men Wales has produced its full share. For men of genius during a long period she was celebrated. Her population has not departed across the Atlantic, it remains at home. And a remarkable population it is, a bit crazed, it is true, on the subject of religion [even Borrovians admit that the Welsh were the people " Lavengro " least understood], but still retaining plenty of old Celtic peculiarities, and still speak- ing—Diolch iddo—the language of Glendower and the Bards."

In the heart of this little country, a spot where the visitors crowd in summer, Llandrindod Wells, a Convention was gathered in 1903. Indeed, there had been a previous meeting held in Mr. Robert Wilson's time, but it was not continued. " Mrs. Penn-Lewis, in her ministry amongst her own people, was much impressed " with the suitability of the spot " for setting forth the teaching of Scriptural holiness. Enlisting the co-operation of Mr. Albert Head she was greatly instru- mental in laying the foundation of this yearly Convention.

" The late Dean Howells and many others expressed warm sympathy. The first meeting was held in the Albert Hall, August 3, 1903, the speakers being Revs. E. H. Hopkins, F. B. Meyer, J. S. Holden, and E. L. Hamilton, and the Chairman Mr. Albert Head.

" The attendance was small, but the power of God was mani- fest. It was soon found desirable to ask Welsh ministers to take part and to arrange for meetings in which the Welsh language prevailed. The Revs. Principal Edwards, D.D., Keri Evans, W. W. Lewis, R. B. Jones, W. S. Jones, Owen M. Owen, have taken part. In 1905, after the Welsh revival, the numbers increasing, a lady handed a cheque for £60 towards a tent—or a site for it—the late Mr. John Cory kindly undertaking the cost of the tent itself (£250). During the eleven years God has set His seal upon the gatherings. Num- bers come from all parts of Wales, and many from the three kingdoms, attracted by the enthusiasm and simplicity of the meetings, in which Welsh singing is often a feature. Mr. A. Morgan, The Mount, Llandaff, and Mr. H. D. Phillips, The Vista, Llandrindod Wells, are respectively treasurer and secretary."

In these vivid words our dear friend, Mr. Albert Head, chronicles this fourth Convention of our homeland. May all four abide and prosper, losing none of their early simplicity or fervour, but adding to their faith, knowledge, and to their zeal, a wider interest on the part of outsiders not often found at spiritual gatherings. Changes Ecclesiastical coming to Wales, Political to Ireland and *critical* to Scotland need more than ever the keeping open the way to "the Fountain of the water of life." Surely these Conventions should do not a little towards keeping open that way.

CHAPTER XX

READER'S LAMP AND CLANSMEN'S FIERY CROSS

" Bring the books but especially the parchments."

ST. PAUL.

" We saw one casting out devils in Thy name ; and we forbad him, because he followeth not with us. And Jesus said unto him, Forbid him not : for he that is not against us is for us."

THE MASTER.

UNLESS spiritual movements have behind them the power of the Holy Spirit, they degenerate into formalism. But to neglect human co-operation would be to ensure spiritual stagnation and death.

Keswick has been fortunate in having men who could dream dreams, and at the same time strive to carry them out. One of the channels through which the stream of blessing flowed was the printed word. Volumes, and even series of volumes, conveyed our message ; notably Dr. Andrew Murray's *Abide in Christ* and his other books. A series edited by the Rev. E. W. Moore, and the works of Mrs. Pearsall Smith carried the teaching everywhere. Dr. Dale, in the *last* lecture in his golden work on *The Atonement*, dwelt, in his powerful way, on sanctification. In reply to a letter from the present writer he said :—" It all came to me in solitary hours on the top of my camel in the Sinaitic desert—natural home, as some would say, of mysticism."

Dr. Moule, the revered Bishop of Durham, has laid us under equal obligations by his pen and by his speech, and Miss Haver-gal by her poetry and by her prose. The evangelical houses of Nisbet, Partridge, Holness, Seeley, Hodder & Stoughton and others, publishers of the above and many other books, have all had their share in this gracious work.

But one firm has made the Movement its speciality, calling, and by right, its establishment " Keswick House." Mr. Hop-kin's *Law of Liberty in the Spiritual Life*, Dr. Pierson's books, volumes by George Macgregor, and Dr. Elder Cumming, series of little books by Preb. Webb-Peploe, Dr. Wrenford, Mr. Houghton and Mr. C. G. Moore, the biographies of Mr. Fox and Mr. Paynter from Miss Nugent's sympathetic pen, and Dr. Harford's work, *The Keswick Convention*, were all, we believe, issued by these publishers.

But the Christian public has perhaps learned most from the organ that voiced the great principles for which Keswick stands, *The Life of Faith*. Founded by Mr. Pearsall Smith under the title of *The Christian's Pathway of Power* (*2d. monthly*), it was published by Messrs. Partridge. Mr. Smith handed it to Mr. Hopkins, and his connexion with it continued till a few months ago. Associated with our friend, especially with his branch of the Church Army at Richmond, were Mr. A. H. and Mr. Edwyn Marshall. As they were publishers, their vicar discussed with them the fortune of the little monthly, and in 1883 they became the publishers of *The Life of Faith*—for its title had been changed. The circulation went steadily up. But ten years after, there were tokens that the magazine was losing its grip. In 1892 Mr. Hopkins and Mr. A. H. Marshall were together in Palestine, and, before he returned, the latter had won Mr. Hopkins to the bold scheme of turning the monthly magazine into a weekly newspaper. It seemed a risk, but a bold faith faced it. A small company was formed and the first *weekly* number appeared on July 27, 1892—the Convention month and week. Mr. Hopkins wrote an article with attractive illustrations about his visit to the Holy Land. A catholicity of interests marks the other pages. Sympathy with evangelistic missions and with foreign missions, and with many another deserving cause, foreshadowed larger interest of later years. The circulation reached 10,000, but it fell again to half that figure. Mr. Marshall's idea of " The Keswick Library "[1] to which Mr. Meyer, Mr. Webb-Peploe and others contributed, and also of *The Keswick Week* carried the affairs of the company safely over its troubled waters.

In 1900 the paper was purchased by Messrs. Marshall at a figure indicative of progress, and under the continued editor-

---

[1] One of these little volumes lies before us,—an admirable one, as proved by its having reached a fourth impression,—it is " The Secret of Power for Daily Living," by the Rev. Wm. Houghton, of Exmouth.

ship of Mr. Hopkins, with the devoted aid of the Rev. C. G.
Moore, it made steady progress, and right royally has it adhered
to its early principles.

The Convention meets once a year, and even with the addition of other Conferences in other places, makes but limited
appeal ; but, supported by an organ sending forth its message
every week, it reaps a harvest, it may be, of fifty-fold. The
contents of *The Life of Faith* have widened, but the develop-
ments of to-day are but the enlarged features of yesterday,
and the policy is justified by the rapid growth of recent years.

The responsibility for the editorial contents rests now upon
the shoulders of Mr. J. Kennedy Maclean. But details of
control come under the careful thought of a Board of Directors [1]
anxious for the promotion of spiritual things, and that in the
line for which the Convention and paper have so long stood.
Thanks to the Keswick Trustees, the paper goes to missionaries
throughout the world, and letters received from all corners of
the globe bear testimony to the blessing which attends its
ministry. The paper has done much by the formation of
Prayer Circles, and Bible Study Courses, to call the people of
God to the important duties of prayer and scripture study.

The power of sacred song deserves a passing word. A tiny
collection of *Faith Hymns* was all we had at Oxford. The Rev.
James Mountain, helpful then as organist at the meetings, was
asked to bring out *Hymns of Consecration and Faith.* Under
his editing a larger edition afterwards appeared ; and as time
went on others were called for, and were prepared under the
skilful editing of Mrs. Hopkins. The hymn book has won its
way into thousands of hearts, and nothing is more impressive
than to hear its beautiful melodies rung out from the lips of
thousands in the tents, or sung by groups on hill-side and lake.
Thus Keswick in its literature is a mighty force, and as the
literature spreads, the movement grows, for the two are indis-
solubly joined in holy bonds.

Partly as the result of occasional visits to Keswick, but more
largely as arising from the knowledge conveyed through the
press, kindred movements have sprung up in separate denomi-

[1] Messrs. A. H., Edwyn, and F. H. Marshall, and Mr. Kennedy
Maclean.

nations. The most remarkable of these is the development in the Church of England, remarkable amongst other reasons from the fact that nearly half the speakers and half the audience at Keswick are not on her roll of membership.

A most interesting paper has come from a vicar who has had much to do with this movement, and who seems to owe his interest in it to personal attendance in our tents years ago.

" Conventions," he writes, " more or less after the pattern of Keswick, now the rule in many parts of the Church, had their origin in the Diocese of Lichfield.

" A Diocesan Convention was decided on at a meeting of Missioners held in 1897," one of them reading a paper of suggestions. " The one which commended itself most to the Bishop (Dr. Legge) was the holding of a Convention for the deepening of spiritual life, and he requested the writer of these lines to organize one at Walsall."

" The object is," says the circular of invitation, " to get earnest people—those who are not satisfied with their attainments," and wish for a better experience, " to meet together to wait upon *God* for a renewal of their strength, and so for a more thorough devotion to the service of man.

" For this Light is needed.

" The Vision of what God is to us.

" The Vision of what we must be to God.

" Do we know all we might of what God is to us ? Are there not unsearchable riches yet to be possessed ? Do we realize what is contained in the promise, ' I will dwell in you and walk in you, and be your God ? ' Are we not too often doing what we can for a *distant* God, in place of going forth in the strength of an *indwelling* God ? " Nor are we " doing what we ought for the service of our neighbour, for the salvation of the world. ' The scarcity of high saints causes the abundance of low outcasts.' Bishop Westcott says—' If only a single congregation could enter into full possession of all that lies in the acknowledgment of the Divine allegiance which we agree to profess (e.g. in the *Apostles' Creed*), if we could each feel, and then all act together as feeling, that faith in God as He has revealed Himself, is the foundation, the rule and life of our lives, there would be a force present to move the world.'

" Archbishop Benson says : ' The Bible never imagines such

a being as a Christian, living and dying without making other persons Christians.'

" This Convention is also to bring us into the light of what we must be to God and man, of testing our desire to be the servants of all men.

" Crowded congregations, thronged altar-rails, of themselves prove nothing. What are the communicants, what are the congregations doing in the week ? Are they the light of the parish and its salt ? *Holy Communion means holy communicants.* ' Holiness means wholeness '—love of God and love of man. Is it so ? Were it so, how quickly would it be seen ? It could not be but that flaming coals would kindle others.

" These days are to be with God, in God, for God.

" ' Ye shall receive power after that the Holy Ghost is come upon you, and ye shall be witnesses unto Me.' "

(*Signed*) MELVILLE H. SCOTT, Archdeacon of Stafford,
Chairman.

W. S. SWAYNE, Vicar of Walsall,
C. E. McCREERY, Vicar of St. Peter's, Walsall,
Hon. Secs.

The movement had been so successful at Walsall that, on the invitation of the Suffragan Bishop (Sir L. T. Stamer), a similar Convention was held in Shrewsbury.

" Other Conventions in the Diocese of Lichfield have been held at Stoke-on-Trent (twice), Stafford, Wolverhampton, Lichfield, Smethwick, Leek, Market Drayton.

By this time the work in the Lichfield Diocese had become known, and at a great conference of missioners from all parts of the country, held at St. Mary Abbotts, Kensington, a paper on the subject was read and discussed.

Since then Conventions have been held in the following Dioceses (probably also in others) : London, Chester, Birmingham, Rochester, Wakefield, Ripon, Winchester, Southwell, Gloucester, Bristol, Liverpool (and I believe) Manchester.

It will also be of interest to know that last year the Bishop of Waiapu, New Zealand, applied for information on the subject."

The *Scottish Guardian* tells of interesting Conventions held at Oban. The first in 1902.

" The Convention has helped to prove that the Church can

unite the blessings of ' free prayer ' with the most perfect forms of liturgical worship. ' This Convention,' said a clergyman of experience, ' has been a revelation to me. It shows what the Church *might* do, and it has given me a new insight into her half-hidden power for good.' Precisely! The possibilities are manifold. Why not a Scottish Keswick on Church lines—and at Oban ? "

The following year the Oban Convention was opened by sermons by the Rev. C. E. M'Creery, whose colleagues were Preb. Bolton, vicar of St. Mary's, Lichfield, and the Rev. H. B. Stewart, vicar of Cannock.

The reference to Scotland reminds one, though it was much more recent, of a very weighty Convention held in Belfast, at which a deeply stirring address was given by the Bishop of the diocese, now Primate of Ireland. The Bishop of Durham and Mr. James Crosbie were also amongst the speakers. The latter writes us : " It has been decided, after statements by Mr. Inwood and myself, to form a committee to arrange for the first Convention [1] representative of Christian life in the North of Ireland ; which D.V. will be held at Port Stewart this summer, when it is expected that the Revs. E. H. Hopkins, C. Inwood, Preb. Webb-Peploe, and A. Smellie, with myself as Chairman, will be present as speakers."

But this is a digression, which, however, may be forgiven to an Irishman and a Keswick man.

It would be impossible to note more specially anything like all the Diocesan Conventions. But reference ought to be made to a very large and important one held in Birmingham in 1908. The meetings were in the great Town Hall, but its accommodation proving insufficient " overflow meetings were held in the Cathedral and the Parish Church. But it is not for the mere numbers we feel thankful. . . . It has been a time of much earnest prayer. Each day began with a prayer meeting at 7.30 " [and this was in February] " followed by the Holy Communion in Cathedral, and Parish and other churches.

" Such solemn subjects as sin, salvation, sanctification and service have been ably treated by various teachers.

" SIN : by the Rev. J. R. Illingworth, Preb. Eardley-

---

[1] Not quite the first, as a few years ago members of the Society of Friends and others had one or two gatherings in Ulster.

Wilmot, the Bishop of Thetford, Canon Newbolt, and Canon Alexander.

" SALVATION : by the Rev. G. S. Streatfeild, Canon Randolph, the Bishop of Durham, the Archdeacon of Birmingham, Canon Ottley, and Preb. Eardley-Wilmot.

" SANCTIFICATION : by the Bishop of Oxford (Dr. Paget), Preb. Webb-Peploe, Rev. Hubert Brooke, Bishop Mylne, Canon Barnes-Lawrence, and the Rev. C. E. McCreery.

" SERVICE : by the Rev. Hubert Brooke, Canon Scott Holland, Rev. H. Gresford-Jones, and Canon Walpole.

" The Bishop (Dr. Gore), gave valuable contributions to the subjects, whereby he enabled the audience to appreciate the connexion of thought. There was a mid-day address at 1.20. The area was packed with men, the galleries with women. Canon Newbolt, Bishop Moule, Preb. Webb-Peploe, and Canon Scott Holland gave the addresses on the four days. The Convention closed with crowded congregations in Cathedral and Parish Church."

In noting with thankfulness, this great movement carried out with his customary energy, by the first Bishop of Birmingham, the author will not be supposed to forget or to slight in the least degree, the older Convention held in the same city and the same Town Hall on Keswick lines. He has too many happy memories of that more catholic Convention to give it anything but the first place.

More recently Conventions on Church lines have been held at Chatham, Blackheath, Chester and other places. The latest of which we have information being one at Derby, February 9–12, 1914. It met at the call of the Bishop of the diocese (Southwell), with the following long list of speakers :— The Bishops of Gloucester and Liverpool, Bishop Mylne, Archdeacons Holmes and Gresford-Jones, Canons Green, Newbolt, Simpson, Barnes-Lawrence, Keymer. Prebs, W. E. Burroughs, Eardley-Wilmot, Webb-Peploe, Dr. J. Neville Figgis, The Revs. Harrington C. Lees, C. E. McCreery, A. J. Tate, F. S. G. Warman.

The subject was " God's Redemption of Man." As a prelude to the hymn book there are suggestions such as we Keswick folk are familiar with. Then come " Incentives to Prayer," verses beautifully chosen, " From the Lips of Jesus Christ, from the Psalms, the Prophets, the Epistles." The book closes with " My Resolution,"—a resolution to engage in some form of Christian work—if unconfirmed, to become a candidate—if in need of guidance, to seek pastoral help.

Other churches have not been slow to catch the sparks of the fire kindled on the Cumbrian hills. " As early as 1885," writes Mr. Inwood, " a Convention was started at Southport by the Rev. W. H. Tyndale who had received blessing at Keswick. He was its president until his death a few years ago. I was there three times. The Convention is held in a tent, the attendance sometimes reaches 1,500. In its early days it was addressed solely by Wesleyans, but in recent years it has included speakers from other Free Churches."

As far back as 1875 there was a memorable meeting of the Congregational Union at the Memorial Hall, at which Wade Robinson advocated our cause. The feature of the meeting which lives most in memory was an address by Dr. Dale, quoted on an earlier page, giving thanks to God for the new vision that had come to brethren in Christ Jesus.

In the present century Dr. Campbell Morgan, representing the best traditions of Congregationalism, and with him the Rev. Stuart Holden and others have started the Mundesley Conference. It has points in common with our own, but the *motif* is different—Mundesley is for education, Keswick for edification. Of course, each partakes largely of the character of the other. But one appeals to one order of mind, another to another. God give His blessing to both.

The Baptist Prayer Union, formed by Mr. Meyer many years ago, gave opportunity for teaching practically on Keswick lines. It was our privilege to address such meetings at " John Street," at Winchester and at Eastbourne.

And lastly, to speak of efforts on a larger and more united scale, " THE FEDERATION OF EVANGELICAL FREE CHURCHES " has been by no means unmindful of the spiritual side of things, and this especially since our friend, the Rev. F. B. Meyer, took the helm. Even earlier than that we find meetings not so much of the annual assembly, as of provincial gatherings, indicative of yearning for practical holiness. There lie before us cards of invitation for three of these gatherings, each of

them entitled " Convention for the deepening of spiritual life."
The first is for the eastern counties, held at Lowestoft in June
1905. There were early morning prayer meetings, and conferences on SIN addressed by the Rev. F. B. Meyer and others ;
on CONSECRATION, addressed by Dr. Barrett and Dr. Horton,
who had preached the opening sermon, and ON THE WORK OF
THE HOLY SPIRIT, by Dr. Horton, and Mr. W. R. Lane.

The next of which we have notice was at Wrexham in
October, 1909. Dr. Campbell Morgan preached and presided
at Conferences on The Christ of the evangelists, The Church
according to Christ, and the first chapter of Church history.

A third was at Bournemouth, Dr. J. H. Jowett presiding.
Amongst the subjects were : " The spiritual inheritance of
the Church," " The spiritual impoverishment of the Church,"
and " Consecration for spiritual life, power and service."

That evening Dr. Jowett was announced as the preacher of
the " Convention Sermon."

The Annual Report (kindly sent by Mr. Hirst, the secretary)
presented at Norwich this month of March, 1914, is full of
interest, and that *spiritual* interest. " A number of our Coun-
cils," it says, " have utilised the Quiet Day idea."

The report mentions one at Ashton-under-Lyne " when
about forty ministers assembled in the morning " and a large
number of ministers and office bearers in the afternoon. It
was a " day of spiritual uplift."

" Uxbridge has for some years had an annual Quiet Day of
exceeding great value."

" The Ilford Quiet Day was also very helpful."

The Harrow Council joined together for similar purpose.

The meetings were not advertised, yet many gathered, and
hopes are expressed to make this an annual event. United
prayer meetings and missions are frequent, and *our* old friend
Mr. W. R. Lane is Missioner for the Council, and for South
Wales and Monmouthshire the Rev. Seth Joshua, whose words
must be quoted : " This ranks as one of the richest years in
my life. Hundreds have been snatched as a prey from the
mighty. Apart from the conversion of sinners a great crowd
of backsliders have been restored . . . the greatest joy of the
year to me has been the evident work of the Spirit among the
young. . . . I have done tent work for many years, but

nothing compares with that memorable month at Ton Pentre or Gelli."

There have been united meetings in a number of places, and some of them announced distinctly as for the deepening of the spiritual life.

What is most cheering is, that several of these have been engaged in by members of the Church of England, as well as the other Churches, and that, in some cases, where " united action had previously been almost unthinkable."

The Free Churches of Leicester united with the Anglicans in a week of prayer, the North Manchester Council in open-air meetings. At Horsham, " Special services have been held for the deepening of the spiritual life in conjunction with the Established Church."

The Stafford Council reports similar co-operation for a twelve days' Christian Evidence Mission ; that at Clacton-on-Sea for a united Brotherhood meeting ; at Leeds for a series of lectures. In Liverpool, Bristol, Halstead, Jersey and other places, Churchmen and Free Churchmen united for social work. At Sunderland they have a standing committee of six Anglican clergy, elected by the Ruri-decanal Conference, and six Free-Church ministers elected by their Council, ready to take combined action in anything that affects the welfare of the town. And, better still perhaps, Conformist and Nonconformist Churches in that town held a United Day of Prayer.

Here we have surely an extension of the Keswick spirit, and all the better because manifested in more difficult times and places than Keswick amid the enthusiasm of the Convention. Moreover, when the aloofness characteristic of our Island, and intensified by " our unhappy divisions," is broken down, more blessing from our One Father, may the children of the whole family expect.

One might extend his view across the channel, nay across the ocean, and think of Conventions in many lands and in several continents. Germany has its " Blankenberg," Switzerland its " Clarens," Paris, Berlin and Stockholm have had many similar gatherings ; and last year representatives from Christiania came to Keswick, eager to establish one for Norway. In Asia, Africa, America, Australia echoes of Keswick have sounded and still sound.

Delightful as it is to think of the clansman carrying the fiery cross of Christ and of holiness, through their several tribes, it is more hopeful far when we can see the same object sought by Christians unitedly. As Preb. Webster exclaimed upon the Keswick platform : " It is in *such* gatherings, where we meet in no name save that of JESUS ONLY, that we may look with confidence for God's gift." " It came to pass as the trumpeters and singers were as one, to make one sound in praising and thanking the Lord . . . that then the House was filled with a cloud . . . for the glory of the Lord filled the house of the Lord." " Behold how good and joyful a thing it is, brethren, to dwell together in unity. . . . THERE the Lord promised His blessing, and life for evermore."

As we gaze over these forty years of mercies, in spite of our errors, temptations, falls, we feel (to change the figure of the heading of our chapter), like the great traveller von Humbolt ; who once when crossing the Andes and gazing on the beautiful constellation of the southern hemisphere, exclaimed :—" It is past midnight and *the cross* bends."

Some forty years ago groups of Christians in many lands realized that it was " past midnight." For some of them the day dawned, and the Day-Star arose in their hearts. Multitudes more have come to behold something since of this inner glory, and proclaim to us to-day, the Kingdom and THE KING are coming, " go ye out to meet Him."

INDEX

✷

Butler & Tanner Frome and London

VISIONS;

WITH ADDRESSES ON THE FIRST EPISTLE OF ST. JOHN

BY THE

Rev. J. B. FIGGIS, M.A.

TO WHICH IS APPENDED A

Memorial of his Jubilee Celebration

Held in the ROYAL PAVILION, BRIGHTON, Dec. 6, 1911.

174 pp.   Post 8vo.   **2/6** net.   Cloth.

COMBRIDGE & CO., 56, Church Road, Hove, SUSSEX.
JAMES NISBET & CO., Ltd., 22, Berners Street, W.

CONTENTS.

Visions; or, An Old Man's Dream.
Followed by
Addresses on The First Epistle of St. John.

Memorial Record of Rev. J. B. Figgis's Jubilee Celebration.

WORKS BY THE SAME AUTHOR.

CHRIST AND FULL SALVATION
NEW AND CHEAPER EDITION.
210 pp. **1/6.** Sixth Impression.
S. W. PARTRIDGE & CO.

AGNOSTICISM
96 pp. **1/6.**
MARSHALL BROS., LTD., 47, PATERNOSTER ROW.

Only a few copies remain ; to be had of the REV. J. B. FIGGIS,
38, *Compton Avenue, Brighton.*

HOMELY HOMILIES
104 pp. **6d.** In cloth, **1/-.**
JARROLD & CO.

A few copies to be had at COMBRIDGE'S LIBRARY, 56, *Church Road,
Hove, Sussex, or of the* REV. J. B. FIGGIS, *Brighton.*

THE COUNTESS OF HUNTINGDON AND HER CONNEXION
1/6.

A few copies remain ; to be had of REV. J. B. FIGGIS, *Brighton.*

THE NEW THEOLOGY
1d. **9d.** per dozen.

AS A MOTHER COMFORTETH
1d. **9d.** per dozen.

LOOKING UNTO JESUS
1d. **9d.** per dozen.

CHOSEN, CHERISHED, COMFORTED
2d. **1/-** per dozen.

AND A FEW OTHER BOOKLETS.

To be had at COMBRIDGE'S LIBRARY, 56, *Church Road,
Hove, Sussex.*

NEW BOOKS FROM MARSHALL BROTHERS' CATALOGUE.

RIDDLE, Rev. T. Wilkinson.

The Faith of a Christian Mystic. Handsomely bound in cloth boards, price **2s. 6d.** net.

A brilliant exposition of the Mystic Way, reviewing all the principal literature on the subject at the present time. In an age of ecclesiastical strife, theological unrest, and spiritual superficiality, the affirmations of Christian Mysticism are of the utmost importance.

FINDLATER, Rev. J.

The Eternal Springs of Revival. In cloth boards, price **2s. 6d.** net.

A history of the Christian Church from the earliest days. The author presents his facts in a most interesting manner, at the same time providing much food for thought. A helpful volume for the Christian worker.

LITCHFIELD, Rev. George, M.A.

The House of the Potter. In cloth boards, lettered in gold, **2s. 6d.**, with a foreword by Mr. Albert A. Head.

" A homely volume of sermons, characterized by a ripe spirituality and mellow judgment. Believers of every school will be edified by a quiet reading of these sermons from Sidmouth."—THE LIFE OF FAITH.

BOUNDS, E. M., Author of " Power through Prayer."

Purpose in Prayer. Handsomely bound in cloth boards, lettered in gold, price **2s. 6d.**

" A book to be read, a book to pray over, a book to make one pray."—EXPOSITORY TIMES.

DURLEY, Thomas.

The King's Crown. In cloth boards, price **3s. 6d.**

" For Preachers and Sunday School Teachers who want Sunday School addresses of the very best order illustrated, this book will prove invaluable."—WESLEYAN METHODIST SUNDAY SCHOOL MAGAZINE.

MACKINNON, Mrs.

Hector Mackinnon. Handsomely bound in cloth boards, price **3s. 6d.** net.

The story of the life and work of the Rev. Hector Mackinnon, M.A. Minister of Shettleston Parish Church, Glasgow, told by his wife. Mr. Mackinnon was loved by all who knew him, and this beautiful memorial of a saintly life will be widely prized. The book is well illustrated, including a life-like photogravure.

FENNELL, Bertha.

The Upward Calling of God in Christ. Daintily bound in cloth boards, lettered in gold, price **2s. 6d.**

A helpful volume of Bible Readings on Old Testament characters.

DOUGLAS, William.

The Story of the Church of Rome. In cloth boards, lettered in gold, price **1s. 6d.**

A clear, concise statement of what the Church of Rome really is.

BLUMER, T. R.

Hospital Prayers. Daintily bound in cloth boards, gilt lettered, round corners, price **1s.** net.

An invaluable aid to those who conduct morning or evening prayers in hospitals, for bedside reading, private wards, or sick-rooms.

BAILEY, E, Boyd.

The Author of "The Spanish Brothers." A Memoir of Miss Deborah Alcock. In cloth boards, price **6s.**

TROTTER, I. Lillias.

Parables of Hope. Daintily bound and beautifully illustrated in colours, price **1s.** net.

The charming freshness and originality which characterize all Miss Trotter's writings have already gained for them many friends. In these new Parables, coming, as they do, straight from the field of service, there is a note of hope and encouragement which will be found most stimulating.

DAWSON, Captain W. H.

Gleanings from the Story of Ruth. In cloth boards, lettered in gold, price **1s.** In paper cover, **6d.**

In this helpful little volume Captain Dawson presents in a most interesting fashion this ever-fascinating Bible Story. A charming little gift book.

SURREY, Margaret.

Joana. New Edition. Handsomely bound in cloth boards, lettered in gold, price **3s. 6d.**

A tale of the Crimean War.

KEMP, Rev. Joseph W.

"The Life of Faith" Bible Correspondence Course. The full set of 38 lessons completing the first session of the Bible Correspondence Course conducted by Mr. Kemp in "The Life of Faith." Strongly bound in cloth boards, price **3s. 6d.**

MARSHALL BROTHERS, Ltd., Publishers,

47 PATERNOSTER ROW, LONDON.
99 GEORGE STREET, EDINBURGH.
124 EAST 28th ST., NEW YORK.

TITLES in THIS SERIES

1. THE HIGHER CHRISTIAN LIFE; A BIBLIOGRAPHICAL OVER-VIEW. Donald W. Dayton, *THE AMERICAN HOLINESS MOVE-MENT: A BIBLIOGRAPHICAL INTRODUCTION.* (Wilmore, Ky., 1971) *bound with* David W. Faupel, *THE AMERICAN PEN-TECOSTAL MOVEMENT: A BIBLIOGRAPHICAL ESSAY.* (Wilmore, Ky., 1972) *bound with* David D. Bundy, *Keswick: A BIBLI-OGRAPHIC INTRODUCTION TO THE HIGHER LIFE MOVEMENTS.* (Wilmore, Ky., 1975)

2. *ACCOUNT OF THE UNION MEETING FOR THE PROMOTION OF SCRIPTURAL HOLINESS, HELD AT OXFORD, AUGUST 29 TO SEP-TEMBER 7, 1874.* (Boston, n. d.)

3. Baker, Elizabeth V., and Co-workers, *CHRONICLES OF A FAITH LIFE.*

4. THE WORK OF T. B. BARRATT. T. B. Barratt, *IN THE DAYS OF THE LATTER RAIN.* (London, 1909) *WHEN THE FIRE FELL AND AN OUTLINE OF MY LIFE,* (Oslo, 1927)

5. WITNESS TO PENTECOST: THE LIFE OF FRANK BARTLEMAN. Frank Bartleman, *FROM PLOW TO PULPIT—FROM MAINE TO CALIFORNIA* (Los Angeles, n. d.), *HOW PENTECOST CAME TO LOS ANGELES* (Los Angeles, 1925), *AROUND THE WORLD BY FAITH, WITH SIX WEEKS IN THE HOLY LAND* (Los Angeles, n. d.), *TWO YEARS MISSION WORK IN EUROPE JUST BEFORE THE WORLD WAR, 1912-14* (Los Angeles, [1926])

6. Boardman, W. E., *THE HIGHER CHRISTIAN LIFE* (Boston, 1858)

7. Girvin, E. A., *PHINEAS F. BRESEE: A PRINCE IN ISRAEL* (Kansas City, Mo., [1916])

8. Brooks, John P., *THE DIVINE CHURCH* (Columbia, Mo., 1891)

9. RUSSELL KELSO CARTER ON "FAITH HEALING." R. Kelso Carter, THE ATONEMENT FOR SIN AND SICKNESS (Boston, 1884) "FAITH HEALING" REVIEWED AFTER TWENTY YEARS (Boston, 1897)

10. Daniels, W. H., DR. CULLIS AND HIS WORK (Boston, [1885])

11. HOLINESS TRACTS DEFENDING THE MINISTRY OF WOMEN. Luther Lee, "WOMAN'S RIGHT TO PREACH THE GOSPEL; A SERMON, AT THE ORDINATION OF REV. MISS ANTOINETTE L. BROWN, AT SOUTH BUTLER, WAYNE COUNTY, N. Y., SEPT. 15, 1853" (Syracuse, 1853) bound with B. T. Roberts, ORDAINING WOMEN (Rochester, 1891) bound with Catherine (Mumford) Booth, "FEMALE MINISTRY; OR, WOMAN'S RIGHT TO PREACH THE GOSPEL . . ." (London, n. d.) bound with Fannie (McDowell) Hunter, WOMEN PREACHERS (Dallas, 1905)

12. LATE NINETEENTH CENTURY REVIVALIST TEACHINGS ON THE HOLY SPIRIT. D. L. Moody, SECRET POWER OR THE SECRET OF SUCCESS IN CHRISTIAN LIFE AND WORK (New York, [1881]) bound with J. Wilbur Chapman, RECEIVED YE THE HOLY GHOST? (New York, [1894]) bound with R. A. Torrey, THE BAPTISM WITH THE HOLY SPIRIT (New York, 1895 & 1897)

13. SEVEN "JESUS ONLY" TRACTS. Andrew D. Urshan, THE DOCTRINE OF THE NEW BIRTH, OR, THE PERFECT WAY TO ETERNAL LIFE (Cochrane, Wis., 1921) bound with Andrew Urshan, THE ALMIGHTY GOD IN THE LORD JESUS CHRIST (Los Angeles, 1919) bound with Frank J. Ewart, THE REVELATION OF JESUS CHRIST (St. Louis, n. d.) bound with G. T. Haywood, THE BIRTH OF THE SPIRIT IN THE DAYS OF THE APOSTLES (Indianapolis, n. d.) DIVINE NAMES AND TITLES OF JEHOVAH (Indianapolis, n. d.) THE FINEST OF THE WHEAT (Indianapolis, n. d.) THE VICTIM OF THE FLAMING SWORD (Indianapolis, n. d.)

14. THREE EARLY PENTECOSTAL TRACTS. D. Wesley Myland, THE LATTER RAIN COVENANT AND PENTECOSTAL POWER (Chicago, 1910) bound with G. F. Taylor, THE SPIRIT AND THE BRIDE (n. p., [1907?]) bound with B. F. Laurence, THE APOSTOLIC FAITH RESTORED (St. Louis, 1916)

15. Fairchild, James H., OBERLIN: THE COLONY AND THE COLLEGE, 1833-1883 (Oberlin, 1883)

16. Figgis, John B., KESWICK FROM WITHIN (London, [1914])

17. Finney, Charles G., *LECTURES TO PROFESSING CHRISTIANS* (New York, 1837)

18. Fleisch, Paul, *DIE MODERNE GEMEINSCHAFTSBEWEGUNG IN DEUTSCHLAND* (Leipzig, 1912)

19. SIX TRACTS BY W. B. GODBEY. *SPIRITUAL GIFTS AND GRACES* (Cincinnati, [1895]) *THE RETURN OF JESUS* (Cincinnati, [1899?]) *WORK OF THE HOLY SPIRIT* (Louisville, [1902]) *CHURCH—BRIDE—KINGDOM* (Cincinnati, [1905]) *DIVINE HEALING* (Greensboro, [1909]) *TONGUE MOVEMENT, SATANIC* (Zarephath, N. J., 1918)

20. Gordon, Earnest B., *ADONIRAM JUDSON GORDON* (New York, [1896])

21. Hills, A. M., *HOLINESS AND POWER FOR THE CHURCH AND THE MINISTRY* (Cincinnati, [1897])

22. Horner, Ralph C., *FROM THE ALTAR TO THE UPPER ROOM* (Toronto, [1891])

23. McDonald, William and John E. Searles, *THE LIFE OF REV. JOHN S. INSKIP* (Boston, [1885])

24. LaBerge, Agnes N. O., *WHAT GOD HATH WROUGHT* (Chicago, n. d.)

25. Lee, Luther, *AUTOBIOGRAPHY OF THE REV. LUTHER LEE* (New York, 1882)

26. McLean, A. and J. W. Easton, *PENUEL; OR, FACE TO FACE WITH GOD* (New York, 1869)

27. McPherson, Aimee Semple, *THIS IS THAT: PERSONAL EXPERIENCES SERMONS AND WRITINGS* (Los Angeles, [1919])

28. Mahan, Asa, *OUT OF DARKNESS INTO LIGHT* (London, 1877)

29. *THE LIFE AND TEACHING OF CARRIE JUDD MONTGOMERY* Carrie Judd Montgomery, *"UNDER HIS WINGS": THE STORY OF MY LIFE* (Oakland, [1936]) Carrie F. Judd, *THE PRAYER OF FAITH* (New York, 1880)

30. *THE DEVOTIONAL WRITINGS OF PHOEBE PALMER* Phoebe Palmer, *THE WAY OF HOLINESS* (52nd ed., New York, 1867) *FAITH AND ITS EFFECTS* (27th ed., New York, n. d., orig. pub. 1854)

31. Wheatley, Richard, *THE LIFE AND LETTERS OF MRS. PHOEBE PALMER* (New York, 1881)

32. Palmer, Phoebe, ed., *PIONEER EXPERIENCES* (New York, 1868)

33. Palmer, Phoebe, *THE PROMISE OF THE FATHER* (Boston, 1859)

34. Pardington, G. P., *TWENTY-FIVE WONDERFUL YEARS, 1889-1914: A POPULAR SKETCH OF THE CHRISTIAN AND MISSIONARY ALLIANCE* (New York, [1914])

35. Parham, Sarah E., *THE LIFE OF CHARLES F. PARHAM, FOUNDER OF THE APOSTOLIC FAITH MOVEMENT* (Joplin, [1930])

36. *THE SERMONS OF CHARLES F. PARHAM.* Charles F. Parham, *A VOICE CRYING IN THE WILDERNESS* (4th ed., Baxter Springs, Kan., 1944, orig. pub. 1902) *THE EVERLASTING GOSPEL* (n.p., n.d., orig. pub. 1911)

37. Pierson, Arthur Tappan, *FORWARD MOVEMENTS OF THE LAST HALF CENTURY* (New York, 1905)

38. *PROCEEDINGS OF HOLINESS CONFERENCES, HELD AT CINCINNATI, NOVEMBER 26TH, 1877, AND AT NEW YORK, DECEMBER 17TH, 1877* (Philadelphia, 1878)

39. *RECORD OF THE CONVENTION FOR THE PROMOTION OF SCRIPTURAL HOLINESS HELD AT BRIGHTON, MAY 29TH, TO JUNE 7TH, 1875* (Brighton, [1896?])

40. Rees, Seth Cook, *MIRACLES IN THE SLUMS* (Chicago, [1905?])

41. Roberts, B. T., *WHY ANOTHER SECT* (Rochester, 1879)

42. Shaw, S. B., ed., *ECHOES OF THE GENERAL HOLINESS ASSEMBLY* (Chicago, [1901])

43. *THE DEVOTIONAL WRITINGS OF ROBERT PEARSALL SMITH AND HANNAH WHITALL SMITH.* [R]obert [P]earsall [S]mith, *HOLINESS THROUGH FAITH: LIGHT ON THE WAY OF HOLINESS* (New York, [1870]) [H]annah [W]hitall [S]mith, *THE CHRISTIAN'S SECRET OF A HAPPY LIFE*, (Boston and Chicago, [1885])

44. [S]mith, [H]annah [W]hitall, *THE UNSELFISHNESS OF GOD AND HOW I DISCOVERED IT* (New York, [1903])

45. Steele, Daniel, *A SUBSTITUTE FOR HOLINESS; OR, ANTINOMIANISM REVIVED* (Chicago and Boston, [1899])

46. Tomlinson, A. J., *THE LAST GREAT CONFLICT* (Cleveland, 1913)

47. Upham, Thomas C., *THE LIFE OF FAITH* (Boston, 1845)

48. Washburn, Josephine M., *HISTORY AND REMINISCENCES OF THE HOLINESS CHURCH WORK IN SOUTHERN CALIFORNIA AND ARIZONA* (South Pasadena, [1912?])